VH1 Music First BEHIND THE MUSIC™

WILLIE NELSON

CLINT RICHMOND

POCKET BOOKS
New York London Toronto Sydney Singapore

An Original Publication of VH-1 Books/Pocket Books

POCKET BOOKS, a division of Simon & Schuster Inc.
1230 Avenue of the Americas, New York, NY 10020

ISBN: 0-671-03960-1

First VH-1 Books/Pocket Books trade paperback
printing September 2000

10 9 8 7 6 5 4 3 2

POCKET and colophon are registered trademarks of
Simon & Schuster Inc.

Design and cover design by: Andrea Sepic/Red
Herring Design

Printed in the U.S.A.

Photography Credits: Photofest (pages 8, 66, 70-71,
79, 81, 100-101, 104, 108, 114, 117, 118); Michael
Ochs Archives.com (pages 12, 26, 30, 52, 74, 76);
Stephanie Chernikowski/Michael Ochs Archives.com
(page iv); Chuck Krall/Michael Ochs Archives.com
(page 110); Jan Jenson/Michael Ochs Archives.com
(page 124); Danny Clinch (back cover, page 58);
Everett Collection (front cover, pages 107, 130); Dan
Connolly/Liaison Agency (page 102); Derek Ridgers
/London Features Int'l (page 84); Dennis Van Tine
/London Features Int'l (page 96); John Reggero
/London Features Int'l (page 129); Bettman/CORBIS
(pages 10, 64, 132, 134); Doug Berry/CORBIS (page
54); Globe, Inc. (page 51); Rick Henson/Rick Henson
Photography (pages 78, 127, 136).

Footage Stills from Farm Aid courtesy of Farm Aid

Additional photography provided by: Lana Nelson,
Connie Nelson, Melinda Swearington, and
Mildred Wilcox.

Lyrics:
"I'm Waiting Forever" by Willie Nelson
© 1996 Warner-Tamerlane Publishing Corp. (BMI) &
Act Five (BMI) All rights administered by Warner-
Tamerlane Publishing Corp. All rights reserved. Warner
Bros. Publication U.S. Inc. Used by permission.

"On the Road Again" by Willie Nelson
© 1976 EMI Longitude Music. All rights reserved.
Warner Bros. Publication U.S. Inc. Used by permission.

"Crazy" by Willie Nelson
© 1961 Sony/ATV Songs LLC (Renewed). All rights
administered by Sony/ATV Music Publishing, 8 Music
Square West, Nashville, TN 37203. All rights reserved.
Used by permission.

"Hello Walls" by Willie Nelson
© 1961 Sony/ATV Songs LLC (Renewed) All rights
administered by Sony/ATV Music Publishing, 8 Music
Square West, Nashville, TN 37203. All rights reserved.
Used by permission.

VH1 Music First BEHIND THE MUSIC™

WILLIE NELSON

CLINT RICHMOND

NELSON'S ROOTS RUN DEEP IN THE GOOD EARTH, AND NO MATTER HOW HIGH HE CLIMBS, HIS FEET ARE ALWAYS PLANTED THERE.

The strangers arrived in San Marcos, Texas, in pickup trucks and sedans, coated in mud from the slush of melting snow along the miles of highway they had traveled. As they assembled at the massive old limestone-and-brick Hays County courthouse, the gathering resembled a scene from some bygone Western movie.

The faded jeans with fleece-lined denim coats, the wind and sunburned faces, immediately identified these folks as farmers, or at least men who toiled out-of-doors in all seasons. They came together in a group below the front steps of the historic, Victorian-style government building, with its giant copper domes and imposing, three-story stone columns. The massive aging structure seemed as stern and unforgiving as the occasion.

The men, some getting on in years, had drifted into the Central Texas town the day before, to be sure they weren't late for the event. Almost unnoticed, they had checked into cheap motel rooms out on the interstate. Someone later said there were about thirty-five of the out-of-towners there that day. By their license plates, it appeared they had come from every one of the states in America's Breadbasket, as far away as South Dakota. A couple of men in the group, the business reps, wore suits and ties. Most were just plain dirt farmers, set out on a determined mission. Their weather-worn work clothes said they had come to town with a definite "attitude."

On that day, January 31, 1991, the U.S. Internal Revenue Service had a particularly attractive piece of farm property going on the auction block.

It was a forty-four-acre farm with a comfortable homestead and outbuildings, located near Dripping Springs, in the Texas Hill Country. The farm was situated in the prime development corridor of what was coming to be known as Silicon Gulch, the high-tech boom belt running from San Antonio to Austin.

An unusually bitter wind caused both outlanders and locals to turn up the collars of whatever type of coat they were wearing as they waited for the government auctioneer to get started on the day's list of seized properties. The towering pecan trees, long sheared by the winter wind of their thick, high foliage, offered no protection from the cold morning. The winter-dormant courthouse lawn, which would be lush and green next spring, crunched beneath their boots and high-top work shoes as they formed a wide circle of bodies close up to the courthouse steps.

As the hour of the auction approached, a larger crowd slowly gathered. The visitors mingled reluctantly with arriving citizens from around Central Texas. Most of the locals were small-time real estate speculators, hoping to grab up a "deal," as they frequently did on auction days. The strangers gradually began talking to the land speculators in earnest, low voices. It was apparent that some of the conversations turned to arguments, but the farmers did not raise their voices in anger.

The Hays County Courthouse, with its massive central copper dome and two smaller sentinel domes, had been the site of many land auctions and forced sales since it was erected in 1908. On these courthouse steps, dreams were regularly sold to the highest bidder. The historic old building had, for decades, provided the official stage for melodramas played out, as families watched their years of sweat and tears gaveled away in minutes, to satisfy delinquent taxes or unpaid liens from failed crops.

Ironically, a statue of Lady Liberty, torch raised proudly to the sky, looked down from atop the cupola on the central dome onto the knot of farmers and bargain hunters.

This forced sale wasn't the first to be attended by most of these out-of-town farmers. Many among them had watched helplessly as their own farms or ranches, along with the livestock, tractors, balers—and, more painfully, the homes and the way of life they had known for generations—fell to the auctioneer's gavel at similar courthouses across the land.

While such forced sales are commonplace on the American farmscape, this event definitely had a different element of drama.

The farm going on the auction block for tax debts belonged to Willie Nelson. The ill fate that the famous singer and entertainer shared that day with these farmers focused national attention on this rarely publicized American tragedy. Bad government policies since the 1960s had devastated American farm families, driving them from the land that had been theirs for generations and turning small farms over to soulless international corporations.

Another irony of this particular forced sale was the personal situation of the man losing his farm. In the years preceding the auction, no single American had fought harder than Willie Nelson to halt the crushing machine of economic change and the devastation it meant to thousands of farm families.

The farmers who gathered in San Marcos, Texas, that day figured it was payback time for the years Willie had spent hosting the marathon Farm Aid shows. But Nelson was unaware of the farmers' plans.

John Arens of Arkansas, representing an organization called the American Agriculture Movement, led the delegation. As the auction began, the farmers circulated among the gathered crowd to tell everyone in attendance how much Willie had done for the farmers of America. They didn't mean to intimidate the bidders. The farmers just wanted everyone to know that, no matter how prime this Dripping Springs site might be for a new Austin suburb, Willie and his family deserved some respect for everything they had done.

The auction went very, very slowly, with no bids approaching the minimum set by the government. In the years since Willie had purchased the property when he first moved his family to Texas in the early 1970s, Dripping Springs had become one of the most desirable locations in the booming housing market. The forced sale of the place had been expected to draw many bids.

But the farmers' appeal was heard and no one bid up the price, allowing the delegation to secure the farm for the minimum opening bid of just over $200,000, set by the IRS.

"I told Willie his family didn't have to move," Arens said later in an interview with a reporter for the *Austin American-Statesman.*

After the auction, Arens visited with the country music icon and told him that the farm group would hold the property until Willie could afford to buy it back at the auction price. Willie's daughter and her family, who lived in the home on the property, were told they could stay until the matter was settled.

"Tears came to his eyes," Arens admitted to the Austin reporter in describing the dramatic encounter.

Willie should not have been surprised that he had so many friends, but by all accounts, he was. Nothing like this had ever happened to Willie Nelson. He had always been the one picking up the down-and-outer, writing

NELSON'S COUNTLESS ACTS OF PERSONAL PHILANTHROPY ON BEHALF OF THE FARM MOVEMENT AND INDIVIDUAL FARMERS HAVE PROVEN OVER AND AGAIN THAT HE SHARES THE PLIGHT OF AMERICA'S FARMS AT SOME PERSONAL LEVEL.

a personal check to a fan who needed an operation for a child or a new wheelchair. Willie didn't know how to ask for help, and his close friends and family say he never would have.

"It was incredible, I was overwhelmed by all the attention that these people were paying me," Willie says of this and other events in the aftermath of foreclosures by the IRS to satisfy long-disputed tax bills. "I had envelopes full of money (coming in the mail). I was surprised at the numbers. There were so many."

While it appeared to be a simple "thank you" from these farmers for the country singer who had done so much for the vanishing small American farm family, this unusual collective action by the farmers and their organization had another deeper, if less apparent, significance.

Willie Nelson, by this time in his career, was one of the best-known musicians and film entertainers in the United States. Because of the type of music he played, and the characters he portrayed in the movies, Willie had become a symbol of the blue-collar American, down on his luck. To the working man, he was an outspoken hero who refused to be rolled over by changing circumstances beyond the average person's control. Willie had proven to a lot of Americans, especially the farmers, that he really was like the characters in his songs and movies. He was the embodiment of everyman to millions of Americans who either still eked out a living on the farms or were only a generation or two removed from the land themselves.

Nelson's roots run deep in the good earth, and no matter how high he climbs, his feet are always planted there. Despite the extraordinary mosaic of his eclectic career, that one thing has remained constant.

WILLIE NELSON SHOULD NOT HAVE BEEN SURPRISED THAT THOSE THREE DOZEN FARMERS DROVE FROM ALL OVER THE NATION TO SAVE HIS LAND. AFTER ALL, HE IS SIMPLY "WILLIE"— SIMPLY ONE OF THEIR OWN.

Willie lore has it that he was taught to pick cotton before he could pick a guitar. And like many Willie legends, it is true. He went into the cotton fields with adult relatives as soon as he could walk. Family members laugh about him riding on the full cotton sacks towed by them during picking season. His grandmother sewed a tiny version of the long cotton sack, and Willie learned to fill his miniature bag by the time he was three.

In his interviews with the national media, Willie almost always mentions that his happiest times are when he's working on the land. In all his thousands of published newspaper, magazine, or book interviews, he's never boasted of the bright lights of Hollywood or the fame that his records and sell-out performances have garnered. He'll tell anyone who will listen that he'd rather be tending cattle on his land near Austin or raising pigs and chickens, as he did back on his previous farmstead at Ridgetop, Tennessee.

While music may be in his heart, the travails of the land and its people are ever in his soul. Look closely into Willie's melancholy eyes, gazing from a hundred album jackets and magazine covers, and the boarded-up storefronts of a thousand dying farm towns can be seen. He watched his own hometown of Abbott, Texas, vanish into America's past.

Nelson's countless acts of personal philanthropy on behalf of the farm movement and individual farmers have proven over and again that he shares the plight of America's farm families at some personal level.

Willie Nelson should not have been surprised that those three dozen farmers drove from all over the nation to save his land. After all, he is simply "Willie"—simply one of their own. ★

HE HAS BECOME THE WORKING MAN'S METAPHOR FOR EVERYTHING AMERICANA

He's "the redheaded stranger" with one of the most recognized faces and voices in the world. He prides himself on being a musical and sometimes cultural outlaw, but he once went into business with the U.S. Internal Revenue Service to pay off a multimillion-dollar tax debt.

Sixty tumultuous years have passed since Willie Hugh Nelson picked out his first chord on a guitar ordered from the Sears, Roebuck and Co. catalog.

His struggles and triumphs through those three-score years have made Willie a legend, who has been described by one of his many chroniclers as a "living museum." He has become the workingman's metaphor for everything American—with his life reflecting both the dreams and failings of our society during the last half of the twentieth century.

Now, at the beginning of a new century, Willie is old enough and financially secure enough to slow down and enjoy his extended family of children, grandchildren, and great-grandchildren on his sprawling Texas Hill Country ranch. Yet he is more likely to be found rolling down the highway aboard his tour bus, *Honeysuckle Rose III*, en route to another benefit performance or fan-packed concert.

Willie Nelson is one of the original country music outlaws who defied Nashville's rules three decades ago to cross over into pop and rock 'n' roll. The American music scene and most contemporary musicians are richer for his daring; and his extraordinary achievements as both singer and songwriter have opened new venues to the present generation of musicians in both country and popular music.

He has written dozens of chart-topping songs in both musical genres, released more than two hundred albums, played starring or cameo roles in thirty movies and documentaries, and won nearly every music award America has to offer, in every field he has chosen to enter.

His live performances are sold out around the world, with crowds of loyal fans following

WILLIE NELSON IS ONE OF THE ORIGINAL COUNTRY MUSIC OUTLAWS WHO DEFIED NASHVILLE'S RULES THREE DECADES AGO TO CROSS OVER INTO POP AND ROCK 'N' ROLL.

him to his shows and concerts. Yet Willie remains just "Willie" (his real name), a humble man who has rarely met an underdog he would not adopt or a cause he would not champion. He is the best friend the American farmer ever had, with his Farm Aid benefits raising millions of dollars each year.

Willie Nelson is more than just the sum of his musical success. In his eclectic life he made his fame and fortune as a songwriter, guitar-picker, singer, and movie actor. But he's also known common labor, having tried his hand as a cotton picker, airman, encyclopedia salesman, Bible salesman, pig farmer, cattle rancher, saddle-maker, plumber, vacuum-cleaner salesman, and disc jockey.

He has tasted life from the bottom to top, down again, and back up. Since fleeing the farm

in his teens, he has experienced huge and heady career successes, rock-bottom ruin and tax debt, recording busts to chart-breaking singles and albums, and a life mixed with personal blessings and heartbreaking tragedy. His downs have been so low they would have destroyed lesser men, but Willie has come back time and again, a reinvented, reinvigorated man on a mission.

Along the way, this "stranger" has shared the whole range of his emotional roller-coaster ride with America through his songs. Many of his greatest hits have been identified as autobiographical—written and performed to amplify incidents from his own life.

"On the Road Again" is the theme song from his largely autobiographical movie, *Honeysuckle Rose*. The lyrics surely represent

IT TOOK A LIFETIME OF **HARD WORK,** LIBERALLY SPRINKLED WITH PURE OLD-FASHIONED TENACITY, TO GRADUALLY EARN HIM THE RECOGNITION OF THE ENTERTAINMENT INDUSTRY IN THE FORM OF HONORS **AND AWARDS.**

one of his most concise descriptions of a large part of his life:

> On the road again
> I just can't wait to get on the road again
> The life I love is making music with
> my friends
> I just can't wait to get on the road again.

Other songs that have stirred millions of Americans are not so lighthearted, but are nevertheless a big part of Willie Nelson. Fans and friends have opined that "She Is Gone" was a lament over the death of his mother. "Angel Flying Too Close to the Ground" is often seen as a grief-filled response to the tragic death of his son. Willie Nelson's stoic, weathered face rarely reveals his inner feelings. Since he almost never speaks of such personal tragedies, many suspect that his songs are his only expressions of his own heartbreaks. And his music speaks the language of everyman, telling stories of success and failure, joy and sorrow, love and loss.

Like one of his early idols, Frank Sinatra, whose radio crooning inspired Willie in his youth, Nelson can say "I did it my way." His lifestyle has sometimes been controversial. But he has remained too close to the Protestant, common-man roots of his upbringing to go too far astray for too long.

After finishing an exhausting performance, Willie—much to the chagrin of his entourage—frequently delays the departure of his crew to wade into the audience, spending long periods listening to the problems and hopes of his fans.

For all his fame, Willie was no instant success. It took a lifetime of hard work, liberally sprinkled with pure old-fashioned tenacity, to gradually earn him the recognition of the entertainment industry in the form of honors and awards. But once his musical genius was finally acknowledged, his lofty place in American music has endured.

Even though his talents as a songwriter had gained the respect of his peers, recognition of his contribution was slow in coming. In 1973, Willie was inducted into the Songwriters Association Hall of Fame in Nashville. He was forty years old and had been writing and performing songs for more than two decades. *Billboard* did not select him as a top album artist until 1976, twenty years after he cut his first record.

The prestigious National Academy of Recording Arts & Sciences has awarded Willie five Grammys® for best recordings in various country music categories. The Academy also presented Nelson with its Living Legends Award.

Closer to home, Willie has received seven annual awards for singles, duets, or albums from the Country Music Association, and has, on one occasion, been named CMA's Entertainer of the Year.

The Academy of Country Music also named him entertainer of the year and has awarded Nelson six of its top annual awards for singles or albums.

Perhaps more meaningful than all the others was the recognition that Willie Nelson attained at the age of sixty, when he was inducted into the Country Music Hall of Fame, joining many of the legendary greats and music-makers who had influenced his own contributions to America's music.

But it was not always so for the redheaded stranger from a tiny farming town in Central Texas. Willie was not born with a silver spoon in his mouth, nor surrounded by anything like the bounty of platinum and gold records that would hang on his walls someday. ★

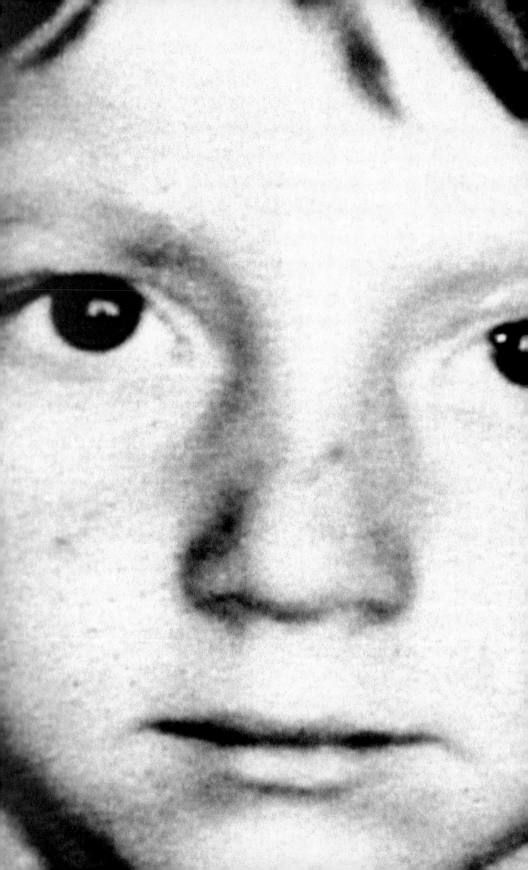

WILLIE DID NOT KNOW IT THEN, BUT THIS NOMADIC EXISTENCE WAS TO CONTINUE FOR THE REST OF HIS LIFE.

illie Hugh Nelson was born poor on April 29, 1933, in the heart of Depression-wracked farm country. But from his earliest days a rich family tradition of music softened the bitter edges of poverty.

The Nelson clan had migrated to Abbott, Texas, from Arkansas in 1929, in a Model-T Ford. Like many other rural Americans in those Depression years, they went in search of a simple living from the land. When the hardscrabble, red clay hills of Arkansas were depleted and could no longer support cash crops, those families dependent on farming had no choice but to move on.

Cotton was the main source of cash in Central Texas when the Nelsons arrived, and

every family's livelihood was in some way tied to that crop.

The patriarch of the extended Nelson family was Willie's grandfather, whom everyone called "Daddy." He was a blacksmith who shod draft animals and fixed farming equipment from his small smithy located on the edge of Abbott. Horses and mules were gradually being replaced by tractors as the power source to pull plows. But work animals remained a necessity on the farm because of hard times during the Depression and fuel shortages in the early years of World War II.

Willie's father, Ira Nelson, followed in his

own father's footsteps and became a mechanic by trade, except he worked on cars and tractors instead of horses and plows. Ira and his wife, Myrle, were still in their teens when their son Willie was born.

Abbott, located twenty miles north of Waco, was in the middle of a fertile region called the blackland prairie for its dark, gumbolike earth. Its rolling, windswept plain had few trees, and those were planted around homesteads and along the main streets of the small settlements. Dirt-poor farmers and petty stockmen and their families, not the cattle barons and cowboys of Texas legend, made up the population that Willie knew as neighbors. Their music was country—bluegrass, Western, and polka—produced from the strings of banjos, fiddles, and guitars. On Sunday, Southern gospel songs provided the inspiration to sustain them through the hard week ahead.

Everyone in the Nelson family, and most of the other families thereabouts, turned to picking cotton at the end of each summer to earn the extra cash needed to survive the rest of the year. The always-hard life on the farm, made even harder by the Depression, demanded that everyone help with the chores. Even as a child, Willie did his share. This demanding way of life was ingrained in his development from his earliest days, and the work ethic would later serve him well in life and career. But, according to an older cousin, Mildred Wilcox, "little Willie never did like to pick cotton," and the experience offered a strong motivation to take a different path in life.

Willie was only six months old when his attractive, nineteen-year-old mother left their tiny town looking for a future with more promise. She took off for the Pacific Northwest in search of a job. Soon after, Willie's father moved away, too, leaving the infant and his sister, Bobbie, who was two years older, in the

"Daddy" and "Mamma" Nelson

care of their paternal grandparents. An extended family of aunts and older cousins helped raise the children.

Grandfather Nelson and Willie's grandmother, called "Mamma" by all the children in the family, formed the rock-solid foundation for the extended family. They were the role models who instilled in the younger generations a powerful sense of right and wrong. But they enforced the family rules with love and compassion. There was no physical punishment required, because the family patriarch's steady and stern voice was enough to settle any issue that might arise.

The grandparents were mainstays of the local Methodist church and they provided most of the Sunday music. Mamma Nelson played piano and organ at the church, and the rest of the family sang. The church was central to community life, and even though Abbott's population numbered just over three hundred, the town had four Protestant churches.

The family piano was not considered a luxury but a necessity in the Nelsons' modest home. Mamma Nelson gave piano lessons to Willie's sister, Bobbie, and other young girls in

the community. As soon as Willie could sit on the piano stool, his sister was teaching him to read music, too.

The grandfather was also a musician who played mandolin and guitar.

Even though the rules were strict and the money was short, there was no lack of love and warmth in the Nelson home. Bobbie and Willie were surrounded by a large family, which provided plenty of old-fashioned nurturing.

Willie's grandfather bought him a mail-order guitar when he was little more than a toddler and taught him his first chords. Willie's grandmother also recognized that he had an exceptionally fine voice. Even when he was a small child, Mamma Nelson fussed over him when he caught colds, taking special precautions to protect his voice from heavy coughs.

Before Willie started grammar school he was writing poetry, an early indication of what was to come later in his songwriting. The words just seemed to flow naturally. As he recalled years later, "I guess I was writing poems when I was four or five years old, things I knew nothing about—broken hearts, love affairs . . ."

WILLIE'S GRANDFATHER BOUGHT HIM A MAIL-ORDER GUITAR WHEN HE WAS LITTLE MORE THAN A TODDLER AND TAUGHT HIM HIS FIRST CHORDS

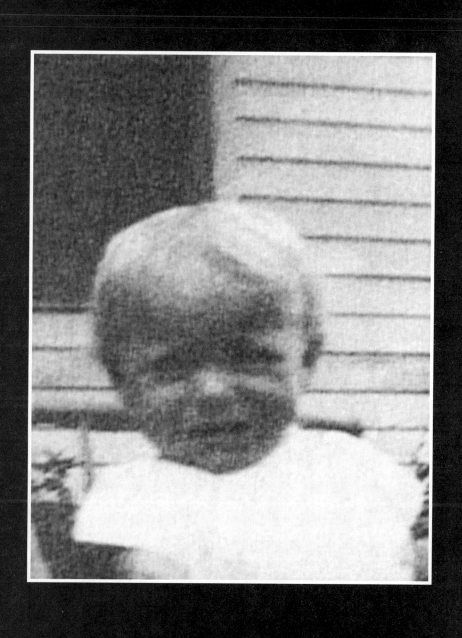

Even though the redheaded boy was surrounded by caring family members, the loss of his birth mother and father had a powerful impact on him. He grew up seemingly happy and was a typical rough-and-tumble boy, like all the others on that Texas prairie. But he missed having a mom and dad.

"The experience of being raised without parents is a fate worse than death," he has said about this early disappointment in life.

But a greater tragedy was to descend on young Willie and the whole Nelson family. His grandfather, a large, robust man who was loved by nearly everyone in the community and worshiped by the family, was stricken with pneumonia in 1939. Unable to tolerate the prescribed treatment, he died after a short illness. Willie was only six years old; Bobbie was eight.

The sudden death and loss of this second father figure in the short span of his life devastated Willie. Already a musically precocious child, he aged faster than his years. He filled the emotional void with music. Every waking hour away from school and chores was spent listening to the country singers on the radio or practicing his own musical skills. By the age of ten, Willie was accomplished enough on the guitar to get part-time jobs filling in as a guitar player and singing with local bands. He and his sister, along with his grandmother and other relatives, still provided most of the music for Abbott's church services each Sunday. But with "Daddy" Nelson gone, the young Willie began to realize that he had a responsibility to earn money for the family.

When Willie was twelve, he landed a job as a substitute guitarist in a Czech-American country band called John Raycjeck's Bohemian Polka Band. He was now regularly augmenting the family's income with money he made performing at local dances.

By all accounts, Willie was otherwise one of the boys, popular and doing well in school, playing baseball, and skinny-dipping with the gang in the pond. But unlike his playmates, Willie was growing up fast, and he spent a lot more time with adults than most boys care to do. He had learned to play dominoes with the old-timers in front of the Abbott general store and seemed equally at home with the older men as with his peers.

He gravitated toward the serious pursuit of earning a living when other boys were still playing games. It was not uncommon for Willie to bring as much as $40 a week to his grandmother, earned from playing in the polka band. That was a sizeable amount of money in rural Texas in those days.

He began building a dream for his future—honing his musical skills, playing in a dance band, and writing music. His songwriting talent was obviously way ahead of his years. He wrote

"The Storm Has Just Begun" when he was twelve years old. The passionate lyrics seemed to reach beyond a preteen's sensibilities, tackling heartache and despair in a sophisticated and mature manner.

If his religiously devout grandmother was proud of this red-haired, blue-eyed boy with a golden voice, she also fretted about his ambition to be a musician. She warned him about a career in music, saying, "Enjoy your music . . . and play it, but don't ever go on the road with it, 'cause that's a rough life."

In a way, Willie was already "on the road," though only a few miles from home. The Raycjeck band played dances in local halls around the town of West, a larger community ten miles south of Abbott. West was founded by Czechoslovakian immigrants who came to Texas directly from Europe before the turn of the century. The beer hall was a part of that community's tradition. But his grandmother and aunts were worried about young Willie's exposure to the dance halls.

Willie, by this time, had already determined what he wanted to do with his life.

He politely argued with the elderly women raising him that he could bring home more money playing in a band than doing chores on the surrounding farms. Clearly, the aspiring young musician had made up his mind that he was going to sing for a living and pick a guitar rather than pick cotton in the hot Texas sun.

Sister Bobbie, still in her teens, married a musician, Bud Fletcher, and Willie was invited to join Fletcher's country music band. His sister played piano; Willie took a spot as a guitarist. The band enjoyed a degree of local success playing dance halls around Central Texas, including Waco, the biggest town in the area. Willie was only thirteen when he joined his brother-in-law's band. He was already a seasoned performer.

Willie graduated from Abbott High School in 1951, and like many young men from the farm country, itched to see some of the world.

Willie with Lana

When the Korean War broke out, he joined the United States Air Force. He served nine months' duty during the early stages of the Korean War mobilization, but was discharged after an Air Force doctor detected a chronic back aliment.

He returned to Abbott and enrolled at Baylor University. With the Korean War GI Bill available to pay for his education, Willie considered seeking a career in agriculture business. But the lure of music was too great. After a brief time in college, he was back playing the honky-tonk circuit with country bands.

It was on the road for one of those dance-hall engagements in Waco that Willie met a girl who was to have a big influence on his life. After a performance, he and a buddy from the band stopped for hamburgers at a local drive-in. Their waitress was a beautiful, dark-haired local girl. By all accounts it was love at first sight, and Willie immediately asked her on a date.

Willie fell head over heels for Martha Jewel Matthews. After first rebuffing the persistent young singer and guitar picker, Martha finally agreed to date him. When they married in February 1952, she was sixteen and Willie was eighteen years old.

Willie kept playing with local country bands, but with a new wife and new responsibility he also needed a more reliable source of income. In 1953, he discovered a line of work that was a natural extension of his musical interest. Willie auditioned for and landed a job as a disc jockey at a small radio station specializing in country music. He would pursue this avocation off and on for the next several years in San Antonio and Fort Worth, Texas. By day, he spun records, sang on the radio, and chatted about music. At night and on weekends, he played and sang in country bands.

Within a year of the wedding, Willie and Martha had their first child, a daughter named Lana. Early marriage and a new baby to support sent Willie in search of financial opportunity. As his mother, Myrle, had done years before, Willie headed west. But there was a major difference: Willie would not leave his new family behind. His quest for work took him and his young family on the road for the first time. Willie did not know it then, but this nomadic existence was to continue for the rest of his life. With Martha and baby Lana, he worked in California and Oregon and landed for a longer stay in Vancouver, Washington, a lumber-industry city across the Columbia River from Portland, Oregon. Willie's mother, who had left the family when he was still an infant, had remarried and moved to that part of the country.

He continued to work day jobs as a deejay and play nightclub engagements with local country bands on weekends. Willie's audiences were now lumberjacks instead of cowboys, but the country music was the same.

"I wanted the job as a deejay because it kept me real close to the music business," Willie recalls. "You knew where all the clubs were and could plug your own dates on the air."

Willie also continued to write songs. Driving to and from the station, he worked tunes and lyrics in his head and scribbled notes on any available scrap of paper. There was no downtime for the ambitious young musician. He wrote such future country classics as "Funny How Time Slips Away" and every verse of "Night Life" while driving in his car.

It was this exposure to the world of professional music as a disc jockey that provided him a glimmer of the potential for a career in entertainment.

At one of the radio stations where he worked, Willie met Mae Axton, who had written the Elvis hit "Heartbreak Hotel" and other successful songs.

"I had some songs, so I asked her if she could listen to a few of them," Willie says. She agreed and set up an informal audition.

"When he played I thought my chin would drop through the proverbial floor," Axton recalls. "I couldn't believe what I was hearing from this scrawny kid."

Axton enthusiastically encouraged Willie to do something with his unusual talent. She told the young father and country deejay that with his songwriting, singing, and picking ability, there was only one thing for him to do: "Go to Nashville!"

But Willie had a family to take care of and no way to get the money to drop everything and head for that magic city where country music stars were born. ★

AT TWENTY-SEVEN YEARS OF AGE, WILLIE HUGH NELSON HEADED OUT FOR NASHVILLE, TENNESSEE.'

orking at a local radio station in Vancouver, Washington, a timber and wood products center on the mighty Columbia River in 1956, the entrepreneurial Nelson decided he would not wait to be discovered.

WILLIE'S DREAMS OF STORMING NASHVILLE SEEMED TO BE SLIPPING FARTHER AND FARTHER AWAY AS THE FINANCIAL DEMANDS OF PARENTHOOD INCREASED.

Willie formed a small band and convinced the station's owner to allot him a half-hour, live-music show. He also made his first recording, using equipment at the small radio station. He cut the single "No Place for Me," with a song called "Lumberjack" on the flip side.

Willie sold the tunes over the air, taking advantage of his deejay job to hawk his own records at a dollar apiece. The clean-cut young singer even threw an autographed photo into the deal.

But limited sales did not do much to change his dire financial situation. Times were tough, and money worries made for a pretty rocky family life. Willie was already spending many of his off-hours away from home, playing the dance halls. Some of his gigs were paying him practically nothing, but his ambition to make it in the entertainment field drove him on.

With a wife and baby daughter, and another child on the way, he felt enormous pressure to give up on music as a way to earn a living. There were nights when his share of the take for a performance was as little as fifty cents.

As in many young marriages with the responsibility of children, money problems led to other problems, and Willie and the strong-willed Martha began to have frequent arguments about their predicament.

"I knew I could make a living in Texas," he recalls of those troubled times.

In 1957, he returned to the state of his birth, vowing to get a regular job that would bring a steady salary. Back in Fort Worth he tried several dead-end jobs outside the music field. He worked as a door-to-door salesman of encyclopedias, Bibles, and vacuum cleaners. But he was unable to stay far from the music he loved, seeking out every opportunity to continue playing with local bands.

The family settled into a routine. Willie actually taught Sunday school for a while, until someone complained about a Sunday school teacher who played at beer halls on Saturday night. He was given a choice of leaving the night work or the church. Willie chose his music.

In 1958, he moved the family to Houston, which in the late 1950s was the oil finance capital of the world and one of the fastest-growing cities in America. Willie joined a local country music band formed by Larry Butler, and continued struggling to make a name for himself. He also continued writing songs. He was now back among aspiring country music pickers and singers, most of whom were not making it to the big time any faster than Willie.

His determination to earn a living and survive as a musician only made matters worse in his troubled marriage. Willie admitted, years later, that he did not really know how to be a husband and father.

Although friends and a growing following of fans kept telling him he should be in Nashville, not Texas, there was never enough money left over to take his talent to the capital of country music. In fact, there was often too little to cover basic expenses. The family occasionally was forced to flee the place they were living when the rent came due on the first of the month.

His daughter Lana, then a preschooler, remembers, "For a long time I thought everybody moved at night. I'd just sit in the middle of the room and watch them [her parents] pack things up."

Willie admits, "I had to move the family at night . . . sometimes when the rent came due we'd head out the window to somewhere . . ."

Willie and Martha now had three children to support. The couple had their second child, another daughter, Susie, in 1957. A son,

Billy, was born in 1958. Willie's dreams of storming Nashville seemed to be slipping farther and farther away as the financial demands of parenthood increased.

He was so broke, that to pay the rent and buy groceries he wrote and sold the song "Family Bible" for $50 to a small music company headed by a struggling music promoter, Paul Buskirk.

"Willie said, 'I've got a song I think you'll like,'" Buskirk says about the transaction. "I said, 'Willie, I ain't got no money. How much do you want? How much do you want before we start?' He said, 'Well, you know. I'll take fifty bucks.'"

"They liked the song and I needed fifty dollars, so, they raised fifty bucks and bought

Susie, Billy, Martha and Lana (l. to r.)

WILLIE SOLD TUNES OVER THE AIR

TAKING ADVANTAGE

OF HIS DEEJAY JOB TO HAWK HIS OWN RECORDS

AT A DOLLAR APIECE

THE CLEAN-CUT

YOUNG SINGER

EVEN THREW AN AUTOGRAPHED

PHOTO INTO THE DEAL

EVEN THOUGH WILLIE HAD MADE NOTHING FROM THE TWO HIT SONGS HE HAD WRITTEN, THE EXPERIENCE MOTIVATED HIM TO RISK EVERYTHING, PACK UP HIS OLD CAR, AND FINALLY STORM THE COUNTRY MUSIC CAPITAL.

'Family Bible,'" Willie says. "I watched it go up the charts to number one—Claude Gray's recording of it. My name was nowhere around. But still, I took a lot of pride in seeing it happen. I felt like if I could write one hit song, I could write another."

And he was right about being able to write another hit.

This time it was a song that was to become one of the best-known country music hits in history—a song called "Night Life."

He sold all rights to the now famous song for $150. "Night Life" has sold more than 30 million records and been recorded by seventy different singers.

After these two songwriting successes, he was still playing with the Larry Butler band six nights a week and working as a deejay on Sundays.

The success of his songs did give something of equal or maybe greater value to the determined, redheaded boy from Abbott,

Texas. He finally mustered up the long-denied confidence to take the biggest step in his young life to date. Still in his twenties, he had a rather large family responsibility. But in the face of heavy odds against him, he knew he had to take the fateful step if he was to ever realize his dream of a career as a professional musician. It must have been daunting, because at the time, nearly every small town in Texas and throughout the South had seen a native son or two pack off to Nashville with his guitar. Almost every one of them returned in short order to take up regular jobs, marry their high school girlfriends, and get on with "normal" lives.

Even though Willie had made nothing from the two hit songs he had written, the experience motivated him to risk everything, pack up his old car, and finally storm the country music capital.

At twenty-seven years of age, Willie Hugh Nelson headed out for Nashville, Tennessee. ★

HE WAS BECOMING RESTLESS FOR A RETURN TO HIS ROOTS.

Willie took to the country music mecca as naturally as a migrating duck to a pond of water. No matter that Nashville was not the ideal place for a struggling young family, he was right at home surrounded by would-be country music artists.

Nashville in the early 1960s was everything an ambitious country and western musician could dream it should be. It was the "big time," where all the important recording studios, music publishers, stars, and the mother lode of country glitter—the Grand Ole Opry—were centered. Nothing happened in country music in America if it didn't happen in Nashville.

And there was a legion of hungry singers and pickers like Willie to swap tales of the travails of the honky-tonk circuit, would-be, should-be song successes, and near hits that had just missed.

Many of these down-and-outers, and some promising comers, hung around a musician-friendly bistro called Tootsie's Orchid Lounge. It was a bar and cafe with rooms upstairs where young musicians could pick and sing. Another big attraction at Tootsie's was the cold beer and hot chili the management provided, frequently "on credit," to the hungry young musicians.

Willie had a few 45s cut by then and a guitar case stuffed with songs he had written on any scrap of paper that might be handy at the time of his inspiration. He had recorded "The Storm Has Just Begun," the song he had written when he was only twelve, along with "No Place for Me," and two or three other tunes.

It was in this upstairs adjunct to Tootsie's bar that a fateful, impromptu audition took place. The determined Texan finally found someone who could pry open the doors to introduce him to the right people. Hank Cochran, a country musician and songwriter in his own right, heard Willie playing and singing.

"He sang these songs that just knocked me down," Cochran remembers. When he asked Willie who had written his songs, he was surprised by the answer.

"He said, 'I did,' and I asked him, 'Who you with, who publishes you?'"

Willie told him, "Nobody. Nobody wants them."

"What do you mean, 'nobody'?" Cochran asked. "Would you . . . could you come out to the office tomorrow?"

Willie Nelson dropped by Cochran's place, a country music publisher with headquarters in a garage. He was immediately signed up as a songwriter and was soon introduced to some of the more successful country music luminaries of the period.

One of the first songs he wrote in this new job was destined to prove that a new talent had arrived on the scene.

Willie was picking his guitar one day and crooning the words: "Hello walls, how'd things go for you today . . ."

Cochran said, "What?"

Willie repeated, "Hello walls, you know, hello window, hello."

The veteran Nashville songwriter just mumbled, "Hmm."

But he introduced the song to Faron Young, one of Nashville's biggest stars, and that song put Willie Nelson on the country music map. "Hello Walls" was soon one of country music's biggest hits.

After that unexpected and sudden

The Grand Ole Opry.
Nothing happened in country music if it
didn't happen in Nashville.

success, Willie pulled a whole stack of songs from the backseat of his car. Among the jumbled notes of songs was one he had written in less than an hour. It was called "Crazy."

Cochran listened to it and told Willie to get in the car. He was taking him over to see another top country star of the time, Patsy Cline. Willie was so bashful and nervous about meeting the country diva that he refused to budge when they pulled up to Patsy's house. She finally called to them, "Tell that so-and-so to get out of the car and come in here."

"I wouldn't get out of the car 'cause I was afraid she wasn't going to like the song, and I didn't want to be there," Willie recalls.

But he was selling himself short, as he had done so often in the past. Cline was crazy about the song, and so was country music America.

Soon everyone was singing the melancholy words, "Crazy . . . crazy for being so

lonely . . . crazy for feeling so blue . . ."

Patsy Cline recorded "Crazy," which became a classic and one of the great jukebox songs of all time.

Other hits followed quickly, and Willie Nelson was recognized as one of the hottest young songwriters on the Nashville scene. Billy Walker made Willie's "Funny How Time Slips Away" a big hit. And suddenly the failed door-to-door salesman and would-be country music man was making a very good living from music royalties.

Ray Price recorded "Night Life," which Willie had earlier sold for grocery money while he was still in Texas. But Price offered the young Texan something else he wanted more than money at the time: a chance to get back into the mainstream of live performances that he had loved since childhood.

Willie had never played bass, but Ray

HE WORE SUITS AND MAINTAINED THE CLEAN-CUT APPEARANCE THAT WAS POPULAR IN NASHVILLE AT THE TIME. HE LET HIS HANDLERS DICTATE HIS IMAGE, SELECT HIS ACCOMPANIMENT, AND MICROMANAGE HIS CAREER. BUT HE WAS GROWING INCREASINGLY FRUSTRATED.

Price needed that position filled in his band, the Cherokee Cowboys. Willie jumped at the chance, even though he had to secretly learn to play the instrument before the first performance.

If Willie was thrilled to be going back on the road again, his wife, Martha, was not happy about being left at home with three children.

An already rocky marriage became even more troubled. When Willie came home after weeks out on band tours, the couple fought. Lana, who by this time was old enough to know what was going on, remembers some of the fights.

"They fought all the time," Lana says. "They were either madly in love or totally hating each other. One night I woke up and she was chasing him with a kitchen knife through the graveyard next door. He was jumping over gravestones. He always could outrun her."

Willie also tells of another major tiff following his return home from a drinking bout with the boys.

"I got drunk and came home one night and passed out, and she sewed me up in a sheet," he says. "When I woke up she was beating the hell out of me with a broomstick."

Willie blamed his wife's passionate temper on her Cherokee blood. But everyone else suspected Willie's road trips would have made *any* wife angry.

The trouble at home did not seem to

dampen the success of Willie's songwriting. But he still longed to perform his own music and began making records and albums of his own.

In association with the Liberty label, he did a single with "The Part Where I Cry" on one side and "Mr. Record Man" on the flip side. During this period, Willie met an attractive country singer named Shirley Collie. Together they recorded "Chain of Love" and "Willingly" for Liberty.

There was more going on between the new country music pair than music-making, and musicians in their group soon realized it.

Willie and Shirley, who were both married, had run into one of the road hazards of the music business—they had fallen in love.

"You could just see it," Hank Cochran remembers of the beginning of the love affair.

Nashville was still a pretty small town in the early sixties, and Martha soon heard about the affair. The marriage had been in trouble for years, but this was too much. She packed up Lana, Susie, and Billy and flew off for a Las Vegas divorce.

One thing everyone agrees on is that Willie probably never intended to give up his family, but Martha refused to let him see his children anyway. It would be three years after the separation before Willie saw them again.

"She was so mad about Shirley, and so hurt," Lana says. "He would try to call, but as far as seeing us, she just put her foot down and wouldn't let him."

Willie and Shirley Collie settled into the Nashville life. He bought a small farm outside the country music capital, near a community called Ridgetop. Willie even took up some light farming, raising hogs, horses, and chickens.

"I really just played at being a farmer/songwriter for a while," he says of that time.

He not only continued his successful songwriting but began seriously to pursue his

WILLIE WANTED TO GO BACK ON THE ROAD, WITH HIS OWN MUSICIANS, DOING MUSIC HIS OWN WAY.

own singing career by cutting dozens of singles and albums.

Willie signed a long-term contract with the Grand Ole Opry and gave up the road performances altogether for the mid-years of the 1960s. He also signed on for regular appearances on Ernest Tubb's syndicated television show.

When Willie's divorce from Martha became final in 1963, he and Shirley Collie were married.

After a little time healed the wounds, Martha relented and let the children come back into his life.

As Willie turned thirty, he seemed finally to be settling down.

"We were in the country. We had horses and chickens and pigs, and Daddy and Shirley were in love," Lana recalls. "They never argued. It

BUT HIS CAREER PROSPECTS DID NOT IMPROVE WITH TIME, AND WILLIE'S FRUSTRATION WITH NASHVILLE GREW. HE WAS BECOMING RESTLESS FOR A RETURN TO HIS ROOTS.

was just a quiet, nice, loving environment."

The one thing that was missing for Willie was any real success with his own records and albums. He watched the songs he wrote become big hits for other country singers, but his own recording career went nowhere.

"He was a hell of a singer," says country star Chet Atkins. "He made records, we put them out, and they didn't sell."

Willie toed the line drawn by the recording company. He wore suits and maintained the clean-cut appearance that was popular in Nashville at the time. He let his handlers dictate his image, select his accompaniment, and micromanage his career. But he was growing increasingly frustrated. During this period he released such albums for Liberty as . . . *And Then I Wrote* and *Here's Willie Nelson*. Moving on to RCA he made more recordings, until by the mid-sixties he had released over two dozen albums.

The producers tried everything that had worked for other country singing stars, but the orchestration did not seem to work for Willie. And he didn't like it, either.

"I felt I needed fewer musicians as opposed to more," he says. "The voices, the strings, and the horns were beautiful, but I didn't think that was the way I should be recording."

Disappointed with his lack of success and the overbearing management of his music, he longed for the one place where he had, for more than two decades in his still-young life, been able to express himself best with his music. Willie wanted to go back on the road, with his own musicians, doing music his own way. In 1966, he formed another band and took his music back to the live audiences he loved.

Shirley had given up her singing career to manage the farm and help with the kids, who were now living with Willie most of the time. As

with his first marriage, his tranquil home life began to pay the high toll of the road.

On one trip to Texas, Willie met a vivacious blonde factory worker from the audience. Connie Koepke soon became more than just a fan.

Then one day a misdirected hospital bill arrived at Ridgetop. The contents of that envelope would destroy the bucolic existence of Willie and Shirley, and ultimately start the countdown toward another big change in Nelson's career and personal life. The hospital bill was for services rendered in the delivery of a baby girl. It identified Willie as the person responsible for the payment and, thus, as the father.

"I was at the house when Shirley found out . . . she got the hospital bill in the mail," says Willie's daughter Lana. "When she came back from the mailbox, she was screaming and fighting and throwing things. It broke her heart . . ."

Shirley moved out of Ridgetop and out of Willie's life. Before long, Willie brought Connie and his new daughter, Paula, to live at the Nashville farm. Willie continued his work on the road, while Connie stayed home to take care of the new addition to the family, along with the other children.

But his career prospects did not improve with time, and Willie's frustration with Nashville grew. He was becoming restless for a return to his roots.

An album Willie produced for RCA in 1968 might well have been prophetic. It was entitled *Texas in My Soul.* ★

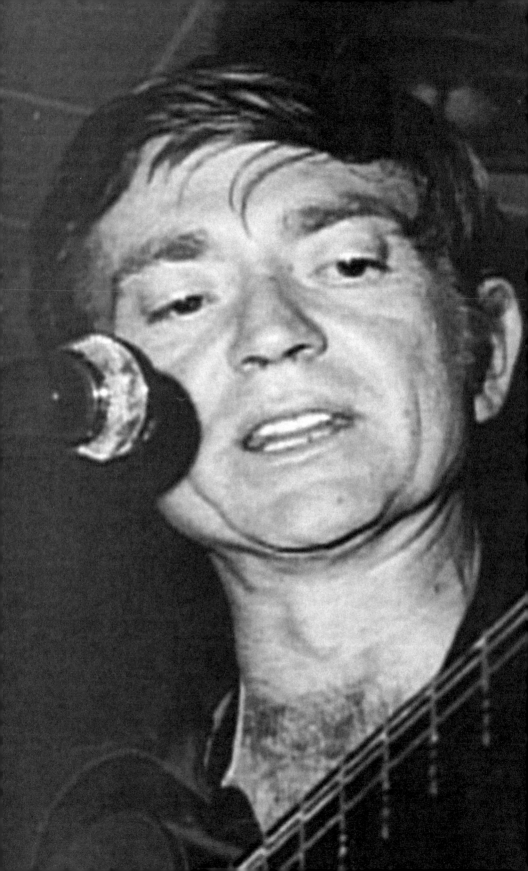

BUT AT AGE THIRTY-EIGHT, NELSON WASN'T LOOKING FOR A PLACE TO GIVE UP AND RETIRE.

By the end of the 1960s, Willie Nelson's first burst of fame as a hot new Nashville-based songwriter and entertainer seemed to be fading.

Even his recordings reflected the turbulence in his life. During this period he recorded such titles as "The Troublemaker," "Laying My Burdens Down," and "Yesterday's Wine." One particular song, "The Party's Over," might have summed up the waning days of Willie's Nashville experience.

Willie formed a new band, which he first called the Offenders and then changed to the Record Men. The group headed west for the Texas dance halls.

It was on the road that he felt the freedom to make his best music. Nashville, Tennessee, may have been where the star-makers ruled, but Texas was where Willie's biggest fans resided. After a while, he and his band spent more time performing in the Lone Star State than they did in Nashville.

Paul English, a drummer who was one of the first of Willie's bandsmen to become a permanent part of his entourage, recalls that it was during this period that Willie began to diversify his musical style.

"We were never really country," English says. "We were just out there playing the music and we never did fit into any mold."

The road, which had already contributed to the breakup of his second marriage, also played havoc with his new family life.

"I think I'm gone too much," Willie reflected years later, still a restless road-bound musician. "I'm not sure they make the kind of woman that would like it. And I'm not sure I would like *her*. I mean, if you've got a gal that don't care whether you're there or not, what kind of relationship is that?"

If this period in his career seemed to be headed for a low point, there was worse yet to come.

"Hank Cochran and I were down in the basement of my house [at Ridgetop]," Willie says. "We wrote a song called 'What Can You Do to Me Now.'"

This lament later seemed like an omen. That night Willie was attending a Christmas Eve party when he got an urgent telephone call.

His home at Ridgetop was burning. Before he arrived, the house, along with a lifetime of his work, had been gutted by fire; what remained had been soaked down by

the firemen. About the only thing he was able to salvage was a guitar case, which legend later whispered contained a small stash of marijuana along with his favorite musical instrument.

Willie is philosophical about the experience. He says, "When you lose everything you've got, it takes its toll in a lot of ways. But in another way, it makes you think that now is a good time to make a change."

On Christmas Day, as he reviewed the smoldering ruins of Ridgetop, an idea began to form in his mind. Perhaps it was indeed time for a big change. Commuting to Texas was taking a lot more time away from his family than was necessary.

All of his friends knew Willie had been growing increasingly disillusioned with the life in Nashville. He still played the conformist role, with the clean-shaven, cowboy-in-a-white-hat look.

But his "outlaw" streak may have begun to show through as he surveyed the visible ruins of the past ten years and thought about his dead-end recording career. He had made a dozen albums and even more singles without one recording ever reaching the charts. Willie was not broke—he still had good royalty income from the songs he had written for others. But he definitely was not happy about his own singing and recording career.

"I just didn't feel comfortable in that kind of situation," he says. "You'd walk into a studio and they'd put six guys behind you who had never seen your music before."

He knew his chances of making it as a recording star in Nashville had gone up in smoke, like the memorabilia in his fire-gutted home.

Willie had come to realize that his handlers in Nashville just didn't understand what he wanted to do with his music.

"I used to think that just because a guy

had a record company, or a guy was a producer or session leader . . . I used to think he knew what to do," Willie says about the last days of his Nashville experience. "He don't know any more what to do than you or me. He's guessing every time. And I realized that. But it took a long time to realize that [they] were just experimenting with me. [They] had no idea what to do with me."

Willie never personally blamed anyone for his failure to make a smash-hit album in Nashville. But he blamed the Nashville clique. And he wasn't the only country musician who was becoming disillusioned with the way things were done in the country music capital. There were grumblings around town about "new breeds" and "outlaws" and "crossovers."

In 1970, a fellow Texas songwriter and singer, Kris Kristofferson, seemed to have kicked over the traces a bit with his highly successful "Sunday Morning Coming Down." The smash hit had all the earmarks of a country song, but it had become a crossover favorite, too. A bigger surprise awaited Nashville when the usually clean-shaven Kris showed up bearded and dressed in casual garb to accept the Country Music Association's award for Best Country Song at the 1970 show.

Other musical events were also beginning to unsettle some of the old traditionalists in American music. In 1971, singers in other genres were starting to break down long-standing barriers between different audiences. Aretha Franklin's recording of "Bridge Over Troubled Waters" and the Bee Gees' "How Can You Mend a Broken Heart" could have played just as well on the country music circuit; and a Western-style folksinger, John Denver, put "Take Me Home, Country Roads" at the top of some of the charts that year.

Country music was still firmly fixed in the old Southern, Protestant traditions from

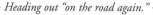

Heading out "on the road again."

whence it was born, but cracks were beginning to show in the puritanical veneer. And Willie Nelson was one of those suffering from the stress fractures.

"It was my fault for thinking [they] did know [what I should be doing with my career]," Willie recalls of his inner turmoil. Like most of his contemporaries, he had gone along with whatever the Nashville record producers wanted him to do, ever since he had arrived in that city in the early 1960s.

". . . That went on for years until I realized that I can do this. I think I know how to get into a studio. I think I know who I want to bring and what I want to sing, and I think I know what instrumentation I want to use on a particular song or album."

But no one was going to let him do it his way in the structured environment of Nashville. And why should they? Nashville was the undisputed keeper of the country music keys. Stars were being born there—using tried-and-true formulas—every day. But many stars also disappeared like novas, after brilliant, short lives.

If anybody thought Willie Nelson was just another nova whose light had about died out, they did not know what tenacity those long rows of cotton and the hot Texas sun had forged into the boy from Abbott.

Instead of trying to rebuild his beloved home at Ridgetop, Willie turned the loss into an opportunity to rebuild his life and career in his even more beloved Texas.

First scouting for a home around San Antonio, he finally settled on Austin. The state capital was less than a hundred miles from the place where he had learned to play a guitar at the knee of his revered grandfather. So it was sort of like home.

And Willie had another reason for eyeing Austin. He discovered a little-known secret, hidden away in the sleepy university city, which

ultimately led him to make his decision.

About this time his divorce from Shirley was nearing a final settlement; he could quickly wrap up his other business in Nashville and make the move.

Austin, at the beginning of the 1970s, was a far different place from the high-technology center it is today. In fact, the population had not grown much in the years following its brief post-World War II boom. Even though it was the seat of state government, Austin took a back-seat to the Texas giants of Dallas–Fort Worth, with their banking, oil, and military-industrial complexes; and Houston, with its international petroleum industry and world-class medical centers.

Several colleges and universities were located in Austin, including the big University of Texas campus in the center of town. In autumn and winter, the small-city population was swelled by tens of thousands of young people from all over the United States and exchange students from countries south of the U.S. border.

Every two years the temporary college residents were joined by an influx of mostly young lawyers from across the state. These career-climbers came to town for the biannual sessions of the Texas Legislature. Some served in the legislature or worked as aides and others wheedled as lobbyists.

These regular migrants also created one major difference between Austin and other small cities in Texas and the rest of the Deep South. Austin was a politically liberal center of a burgeoning, progressive music culture. As early as the 1960s, Austin had been the breeding ground for a growing counterculture of musicians with a large hippie following among the students. Janis Joplin, whose "Me and Bobby McGee" recording was at the top of many of the charts in 1971, had her early start performing at a bistro converted from a gas

station, called Threadgill's. She played with an Austin bluegrass group even before the rock era broke across the American music scene.

Without this underground music culture, Austin would have been just another midsized government center and university town. While it was a picturesque place situated on the sluggish, dammed-up Colorado River, Austin still had little to offer anyone with ambitions for national attention.

It would have been an unlikely place for an entertainer to locate, unless he planned to join the substantial communities of retirees that inhabited the nearby Hill Country. But at age thirty-eight, Nelson wasn't looking for a place to give up and retire. He was looking for something different, and he had discovered

it in Austin's best-kept secret: a musical revolution was brewing there.

Willie discovered the music was hidden away in the smoky beer joints where the students and part-time legislators hung out. Austin was still Texas and cowboy country, so Western music thrived around the city. But there was a different kind of music incubating in these beer joints around Central Texas, and Austin was at the hub of this movement.

The new music was called by various names—rockabilly, redneck rock. It wasn't country, it wasn't rock, and it wasn't pop. And nothing from this emerging style had made any of the charts in 1971. In fact, it would take Willie Nelson's interpretations to bring the genre to respectability.

AND MORE THAN HIS APPEARANCE WAS ALTERED. WILLIE'S MUSIC WAS DIFFERENT, TOO NOBODY SUSPECTED IT THEN BUT THIS REMARKABLE MIDLIFE CAREER CHANGE WOULD HAVE FAR-REACHING IMPACT ON COUNTRY MUSIC AND MUSICIANS FOR YEARS TO COME

The embryonic Austin music scene was waiting for a breath of life from someone like Willie and the band of music "outlaws" he would later draw to the Hill Country with him.

But as a newcomer, Willie Nelson had no such grand plans. He just wanted a fresh start. On April 30, 1971, he married Connie Koepke. Technically, his divorce from Shirley would not be final for several more months.

He had signed with Atlantic Records a short time before heading off to Texas to start a new life. The Atlantic contract included one clause that was a big improvement over his previous legal commitments—Willie could use his own band for the recordings. Nobody at the time suspected how drastic the change would be for the clean-shaven Nashville songwriter.

Once free of the Nashville handlers, an invigorated Willie Nelson literally began to remake himself from head to toe. He took advantage of the still low-priced real estate in the Hill Country west of Austin and bought a place not far out of town, near a little community called Dripping Springs.

He quickly settled into the new life, which was not all that different from the life he had known in Texas before Nashville—except now he could pay the rent on time and his children did not have to worry about midnight moves.

But there was something else quite different, and it soon became apparent to friends and family who had not seen him in a while.

Willie drove to the municipal airport at Austin to pick up his older daughter, Lana. Susie and son, Billy, were already with Willie in Texas at the time.

"He picks me up at the airport and he's got long hair and a beard and an earring," Lana, who was almost twenty years old at the time, remembers. "I'm going like, 'Whoa, now this is a different dad!'"

THE NEW MUSIC WAS CALLED BY VARIOUS NAMES— ROCKABILLY, REDNECK ROCK. IT WASN'T COUNTRY, IT WASN'T ROCK, AND IT WASN'T POP. AND NOTHING FROM THIS EMERGING STYLE HAD MADE ANY OF THE CHARTS IN 1971.

It *was* a different Willie. He had traded the Mr. Clean Nashville look for the hippest garb he could find. Willie was not only red-haired, he was red-bearded, too. His cowboy boots were replaced by tennis shoes, and his Western-cut, three-piece suit by torn jeans, a T-shirt, and vest.

And more than his appearance was altered. Willie's music was different, too. Nobody suspected it then, but this remarkable midlife career change would have far-reaching impacts on country music and musicians for years to come.

With a small cadre of likewise frustrated Western singers who had grown disillusioned with Nashville, Willie led the crossover to an eclectic new style of music. Eventually the progressive country sound would swell the numbers of Americans and fans around the world who adopted "country" music as their own. ★

EVERYBODY CAME FOR THE MUSIC.

ustin was good for Willie, and Willie was good for
Austin. Although he had left Nashville dissatisfied with his career,
Nelson enjoyed a following of fans and a reputation as a major
country and Western songwriter that, by local standards, made him
famously successful.

Among a small but growing group of Western entertainers, the drastic change in appearance and progressive sound in music was the latest trend. In Willie's case, a Western-style bandanna, usually worn as a neckerchief, became a headband; and faded jeans, vest, and scuffed sneakers became his trademark. At his numerous live performances, Willie began tossing the sweaty kerchiefs off the stage to the cheering audience, somewhat like Elvis had done earlier with his silk scarves.

Willie's fans and family, and maybe even Willie himself, did not know that he was about to begin the most prolific and successful period in his musical career. His early Austin years were definitely transitional, and while he was experimenting with new sounds and songs, he also continued to cut albums in the standard country format. There was one improvement, however. He was using his own band for backup.

Even so, Willie's new recordings, such as *Shotgun Willie* and *Phases and Stages*—while well received by a growing army of fans—did not immediately propel him to the top of the album charts.

Shortly after arriving on the Austin scene, Willie happened into a group of music boosters running an unlikely venue called the Armadillo World Headquarters. A strange thing was going on in Austin's largely counterculture music scene, and much of what was happening was centered at a cavernous old building converted from a pre–World War II National Guard armory. A motley beer garden, made lush with a jungle of tangled plants, had been added, replacing part of the gravel parking lot.

Austin and the surrounding countryside supported two distinctly different music scenes at the time. The two were like oil and water. There was still a strong cowboy culture supported by fans from the farms and ranches around the city and bolstered frequently when Aggies from Texas A&M roared into town from College Station to confront their arch rivals at the University of Texas.

Austin's second, and largest, musical clique was centered around the strong hippie and anti–Vietnam War population at the University of Texas and the other colleges and universities in and around the city.

A much smaller and less influential movement had also thrived in Austin for years. This movement featured the blues and spiritual music groups in Austin's eastside

black community. But the real tug-of-war was between the kickers and the flower children.

Hard-core country and Western was the music of one group, and hard rock or acid rock was the anthem of the other. Each had its own hangouts, and one group ventured into the others' joints at its peril.

That is, until the Armadillo World Headquarters came into existence a short time before Willie moved his family and his music to Austin. The music hall was initially opened, or more aptly cobbled together, to accommodate the hard rockers.

Even so, it attracted Willie's attention. The big barnlike, dilapidated concert hall, bar, beer garden, and restaurant was the only place in town where local, live performances were still available to crowds of any size. Officially, the better auditoriums at the universities and colleges were pretty much off-limits, except to the sanctioned orchestras, touring theatrical troupes, and dance companies.

The Armadillo World Headquarters was the brainchild of a group of longtime Austin-area music aficionados, headed by Eddie Wilson. Wilson had discovered the abandoned old building by accident one night when he and his friends stepped behind a skating rink to take

a leak. They spied a sprawling building with broken, metal-framed windows. On closer inspection, it proved to be large enough to house a sizeable audience. Austin had recently lost its only other big venue, a hippie-rock emporium called the Volcan Gas Company. By the time that music hall was forced to close, many of the Austin-based hard rock groups of the late sixties had simply left town, most migrating to San Francisco.

When Willie Nelson first arrived, Austin had only a handful of typical Texas honky-tonks and beer joints where small crowds could go for live music. These were the domain of country music, with a few jazz joints in East Austin for the blues players.

Eddie Wilson rented the vacant armory, spruced it up a bit, and began inviting local groups to perform. He hired an Austin artist to paint murals on the walls, depicting armadillos—those strange armor-plated critters—rushing around in various activities. He named the place the Armadillo World Headquarters. At the time, the lowly armadillo was not yet popularized as Texas's lovable symbol. Most people thought of the pest as a nuisance that rooted up gardens,

AT AN AGE WHEN MANY
ENTERTAINERS
ARE CONSIDERED PAST THEIR PRIME
WILLIE WAS STARTING
A NEW MOVEMENT
HE HAD REINVENTED HIMSELF
AND CREATED A NEW NICHE FOR COUNTRY MUSIC
IN THE PROCESS

or as the strange-looking roadkill seen along the state's high-speed highways.

The big concert hall wasn't even air-conditioned, which, with Austin's brutal heat and humidity, should have assured its doom from the beginning. Patrons had to stand or sit on scraps of carpeting rolled out on the main floor of the performance hall for lack of adequate seating. The carpeting was usually beer-stained and covered with cigarette burn holes and dropped ashes.

The place had a large stage for the performing groups and plenty of room for spontaneous dancing. The funky crowds came for the music anyway, and definitely not for the atmosphere or the somewhat limited menu. Its bill of fare has been described as mainly cheap beer and pot, with leafy vegetarian dishes as the entree.

Initially, the Armadillo was Austin's hippie headquarters, but gradually Eddie Wilson tried to broaden the audiences by inviting different types of musicians to perform. It was not uncommon to have rock, blues, and pop groups playing on the same evening. Wilson even provided a place for the Austin Ballet Company to perform after it had been kicked out of more formal digs for some controversial performance antics.

One day Willie Nelson and a couple of his bandsmen dropped by the big facility to see what all the talk was about. Eddie Wilson was there.

"He walked up and said, 'I want to play here' and I said, 'I *want* you to play here—let's do it,'" Wilson recalls.

Although Wilson was more identified with the rock movement in Austin, he had been an admirer of Willie's music for years.

Willie and his band were booked into the Armadillo between hard rock acts; nobody knew what to expect from the hippie clientele.

When Wilson announced that Willie Nelson would be among the upcoming attractions to play the headquarters, only two or three patrons in the largely hippie crowd clapped. Eddie thought he had made a big mistake. And sure enough, Willie's first appearance at the Armadillo World Headquarters did not draw too large a crowd. But it did bring together a different sort of audience than was usual for the place. That first appearance was attended by between 300 and 400 young people, about evenly mixed between cowboys and hippies.

Gradually the crowds grew, and over the next ten years that the Armadillo remained in business, Willie and what came to be known as country music outlaws were regulars at the sprawling Austin music hall.

But more important than the size of the crowds was the evolution of the sound. Cowboys and hippies, once believed to be irreconcilable natural enemies, gathered together to hear an emerging new brand of music. Austin, Texas, became the unlikely center for a musical movement that melded radically different forms of country and rock, and the cultures they represented.

The music itself has been called many things. Essentially it was merely a new form of progressive country music. Its advent, pioneered by Willie and a handful of other country singers, greatly expanded the American country music audience and helped to create the megastar, country-style performers that were to storm the music scene two decades later.

But in the early 1970s, Willie's revolt against Nashville caused him and his fellow revolutionaries to be called outlaws. There never really was an organization per se, and a number of country musicians came and went through the ranks of the group identified as such. Among the more notable country singers identified with this early group were Kris Kristofferson and Waylon Jennings. The chief complaint against

WILLIE WAS ONE OF THE FIRST OF THE NEW BREED TO RECOGNIZE THE POTENTIAL FOR ATTRACTING DEVOTEES FROM THE BLUES, POP, AND ROCK MUSIC CULTURE TO COUNTRY MUSIC.

the outlaws was their insistence on having greater creative control over their recordings.

Willie was one of the first of the new breed to recognize the potential for attracting devotees from the blues, pop, and rock music culture to country music. But he knew the music had to be more progressive to interest larger followings of new fans. His acceptance by an increasingly mixed crowd at the Armadillo must have encouraged him that he was on the right track.

He also knew he needed a much broader venue than the smoky confines of the old renovated army building. While he continued to support his growing legion of loyal fans with traditional country music at performances in the dance halls around Texas, he was beginning to reach a new and younger audience. He gradually introduced more of the new style of music into his repertoire.

With that audience foremost in his mind, Willie dreamed up a new venue for country

music. If the Haight-Ashbury crowds could support events like Woodstock, why couldn't progressive country also attract such enthusiasm? Willie decided to host a country music festival on the order of the successful rock concerts that had energized young rock fans from the sixties onward. Willie set up a loosely organized picnic and country music event at tiny Dripping Springs, Texas, located not far from his new ranch home in the Hill Country.

The Dripping Springs picnic was set for Independence Day 1972. It was billed as "the biggest country music spectacular ever held."

He got commitments from his old friends and associates from the country music business, including such notables as Tom T. Hall, Tex Ritter, Roy Acuff, and Bill Monroe. Also appearing on the program were many of his more recent "outlaw" friends and country singers who were definitely a part of the music rebellion. Performers included Kris Kristofferson, Waylon Jennings, Billy Joe Shaver, Sammi Smith, and Charlie Rich.

July 4, 1972, was a typically sizzling summer day in Central Texas, and the crowds for the three-day event were disappointingly small. But when Willie held his July Fourth celebration the following year, it attracted more than 40,000 people.

Those who did attend the first event proved their fanatical zeal for the music. They sat in the boiling sun, baking in heat reflected from a white limestone pasture, and heard some of the most revolutionary new sounds in country music. There were plenty of traditional Western entertainers, but the new country-rock sound had its formal debut.

Although the event was a financial disaster for the promoters, this did not dampen Willie Nelson's enthusiasm for the new venue he had created. It had been such a *musical* success that he vowed, along with his gathering of friends and associates from the old Nashville

AS THE EVENT GREW BIGGER AND, MOST IMPORTANTLY, MORE ECLECTIC, THE COWBOY AND "REDNECK" CROWDS REMAINED FAITHFUL. BUT THE AUDIENCE HAS BECOME AS DIVERSE AS THE NATION ITSELF.

days, that it would be an annual happening, to be known as Willie Nelson's Reunion.

It would become one of the most outstanding music events in America, drawing enthusiastic fans back year after year, as it moved from place to place around Texas. The event was staged several years at its original location at Dripping Springs, and then moved around Texas to College Station (heart of Aggieland), Gonzales, Southpark, Manor Downs (a quarterhorse racetrack), and several other locations. A 1975 crowd at Liberty Hill was estimated at 90,000. A 1987 gathering at a long-haul truck depot called Carl's Corner near Hillsboro, just a few miles from where Willie was born, had a paid attendance of only 8,000. Willie reportedly lost more than a half-million dollars.

That one year's disappointing turnout and financial loss would have killed the event for most promoters. Not Willie Nelson. He bit the bullet and came back with an even more impressive Reunion three years later, when he brought the event to Austin's near-downtown Zilker Park. The theme for the comeback was truly "family reunion," but the concerts were now

called "Willie's Fourth of July Picnics."

For the Austin picnic, Willie brought together the old favorites of Kris and Waylon. He set up a separate children's stage featuring jugglers, magicians, carnival rides, and armadillo races. The celebration ended with a spectacular fireworks display. Much of Austin came to sit on surrounding hills to view the fireworks, even if they couldn't get tickets to the jammed main show.

Significant to Willie, however, were the benchmarks provided by the event as a gauge of the acceptance of what Willie and his outlaw cohorts were doing in country music.

As the event grew bigger and, most importantly, more eclectic, the cowboy and "redneck" crowds remained faithful. But the audience has become as diverse as the nation itself. Motorcycle gangs on their best behavior annually join with families herding small children; aging hippies and rockers loll semi-nude among booted cowboys; and Latino ranch workers join happily with redneck laborers. It's a family event with children from all these groups mingling freely, often for the first time in their lives. They all come to hear a

broad spectrum of musical styles, from bluegrass and country to Tejano to rock. And leading the show is always Willie Nelson.

"Everybody came for the music," his daughter Lana says about the live appearances at the Armadillo and the early Reunions. "There were hippies and rednecks everywhere. Everyone came for the music."

Willie had found his own voice, daring to experiment with pop, rock 'n' roll, blues, and any other genre that struck his fancy. *Shotgun Willie* and *Phases and Stages* were the last two albums he did for Atlantic before that studio went out of the country music business.

He signed on with Columbia (CBS), with enough confidence that he could stipulate to that label's management that he would henceforth do his music his own way. He had his own band playing backup now, a band he called the Family, which actually did include his long-loyal sister, Bobbie. Most of the members of his musical family have stayed with him ever since.

The first album he recorded with Columbia was innovative in the industry and different from anything even he had done before. It proved that he had been right all along and launched the new country sound that came to be known simply as "outlaw."

He recorded all the songs for the album *Red Headed Stranger* and presented it as a finished product to Columbia management.

"When we signed him [at CBS Records], he came with a project that was already recorded," said Rick Blackburn, who was president of CBS Records at the time. "We thought it was a demo."

But Willie made it clear that the project was completed—that was it.

"That record is done. All you have to do is put it out," he said.

Blackburn chuckles at the memory.

"If you know Willie, there's no negotiation, there's no more discussion, the case is closed.

Willie told us, 'Put it out and you all have a nice day. Call me when it's a hit.' He went back to Austin and we released a single from the *Red Headed Stranger* album. We didn't think it had much of a chance."

The single was "Blue Eyes Crying in the Rain," a song written by Fred Rose. It featured only Willie's voice, a guitar, and a bass. It was an overnight smash.

"It was instantaneous," Blackburn says. "I mean, nobody was more shocked than we were. It didn't have . . . the bells and whistles. It wasn't the way you went about making a record in Nashville in those days. Just a very simple vocal, guitar, and bass. But it told a story. It's a very beautiful song."

His new record producers were equally surprised by the fans' acceptance of the radical new image conveyed by Willie's long hair, beard, and hippie attire.

"Here was a guy doing traditional country music who was dressing more like the Grateful Dead," Blackburn recalls. "That raised some eyebrows. Nobody could get a handle on Willie Nelson. It was confusing."

Red Headed Stranger became a major hit, climbing to number one on the country charts and residing comfortably in the Top 40 of the pop charts. He won his first Grammy for "Blue Eyes Crying in the Rain." And that super-hit single achieved another significant goal for Willie: It broke down the historic barriers that had existed between popular music and country and was a crossover success.

If he had been spinning his wheels before coming to Austin, Willie found traction just down the road from his old hometown. At an age when many entertainers are considered past their prime, Willie was starting a new movement. He had reinvented himself and created a new niche for country music in the process. ★

THE AWARDS KEPT ROLLING IN.

fter "Blue Eyes Crying in the Rain," the recording people couldn't get enough of the man who came to be known as the red-headed stranger, the title of that hit song's album. Several of Nelson's earlier albums were pulled from the shelf, dusted off, and reissued. Ironically, one old title, What Can You Do to Me Now, *was among those re-releases. He had conceived that song the night before his Ridgetop farm home burned to the ground, indirectly causing him to leave Nashville. His uncanny knack for turning misfortune to fortune had made the move a good one, and Willie finally claimed the success that had eluded him for so many years.*

Willie was now on his way back up with a sack full of new songs. In 1975, the country music industry had to pay attention, and Willie Nelson was singled out for some long overdue peer recognition. Until *Red Headed Stranger,* his only recognition had been his 1973 induction into the Nashville Songwriters Hall of Fame.

In 1975, *Red Headed Stranger* won Willie a Grammy for Best Country Vocal Performance. That album and the remarkable success of the single "Blue Eyes Crying in the Rain" established him as a phenomenal new star in his own right.

Although he was always in a crowd, surrounded by old friends, family, and fellow musicians, he still carried the aura of a lonesome stranger in his performances and his melancholy delivery.

"It was just Willie and the guitar," says longtime friend and frequent co-star Kristofferson. "That was it. I mean that [song] broke down so many barriers. Classical simplicity. It still tears me up."

If the instant hit introduced the stranger to a huge new audience, those closest to him knew that the old Willie Nelson was only finally introducing the real Willie. He, along with other entertainers who had fled the Nashville scene since 1970, had been working hard for years to have their real voices heard.

Two awards in 1976 proved there were no hard feelings by the industry toward the "outlaws" who had fled Nashville to do it their way. The Country Music Association (CMA) gave its Album of the Year award to Willie, Waylon, Jessi Colter, and Tompall Glaser for *Wanted: The Outlaws.* And CMA's Single of the Year went to Willie and Waylon for "Good Hearted Woman."

The *Outlaws* album had gone platinum, and its popularity heralded a new musical image in country music that was to last for more than a decade. The outlaw image brought Nelson and his buddies, like Kristofferson, Jennings, and another longtime Nashville renegade, Johnny Cash, a string of hits and a niche of their own.

Gold and platinum records continued to roll out for Willie, and he took many of his friends along with him on this ride to the top. Some of his album titles reflect his willingness to share the limelight, titles like *Willie Nelson and His Friends, Waylon and Willie, Willie and Family Live, Willie Nelson Sings Kristofferson,* and *One for the Road (with Leon Russell).*

But he had many other solo hits supported only by guitar and bass, and relying primarily on his distinctive, and by now widely recognized, voice. Albums like *There'll Be No Teardrops Tonight,* a remake of *Hello Walls,* and *Face of a Fighter* kept Willie in the mainstream of country while he experimented, successfully, with songs from other genres.

Then Willie startled even some of the people who thought they knew him best. He took one of the biggest risks of his career, right in the middle of his soaring rise to fame and fortune with the raucous outlaw sound.

Sandwiched between a Waylon and Willie album and a remake of *Hello Walls,* he went pop-classical and issued an album called *Stardust.*

"I had been wanting to do that for a long time," Willie says. "I wanted to go into the studio and do *Stardust* and then 'Moonlight in Vermont.'"

Willie was once again about to prove that he would not be restrained by some preordained set of rules written by someone else.

He once told an interviewer that he did not believe there was any reason to "label music" at all.

"I look at it all as just American music," Willie said.

WILLIE WAS ONCE AGAIN ABOUT TO TO PROVE THAT HE WOULD NOT BE RESTRAINED BY SOME PREORDAINED SET OF RULES WRITTEN BY SOMEONE ELSE.

If there were naysayers concerning Willie's venture into popular classics, they were quickly proven as wrong as his earlier handlers had been when they scoffed at his suggestions. The *Stardust* album, with the title song by Hoagy Carmichael, was issued in 1978. It featured such old favorites as "Blue Skies" and "All of Me," and soared to the top of the charts, selling over four million albums. *Stardust* also remained on the charts for an incredible five hundred weeks.

Willie would continue to record duets with country stars for the rest of his career,

singing with such country greats as Merle Haggard, Emmylou Harris, Hank Snow, Ernest Tubb, Faron Young, Dolly Parton, Webb Pierce, Ray Price, and his old regulars, Cash, Kristofferson, and Jennings.

But his choice of other recording partners proved he didn't care for pigeonholing his music. He has recorded duets in a broad range of musical genres with Ray Charles, Neil Young, Bob Dylan, Carlos Santana, and Julio Iglesias.

The awards kept rolling in. In 1979, Willie was named CMA Entertainer of the Year, and he won another Grammy in 1978 as Best Male

ONCE MORE THE BOY
FROM ABBOTT, TEXAS
PROVED THAT JUST ABOUT ANYTHING IS
POSSIBLE IN AMERICA
WILLIE LAUNCHED HIS ACTING CAREER
WITHOUT ANY TRAINING
WHATSOEVER, AT THE TENDER
AGE OF FORTY-SIX

Country Vocal Performer for "Georgia on My Mind." In a show of his eclectic breadth, that year he also shared a Grammy for Best Country Vocal Performance by a Duo or Group, with Waylon Jennings, for "Mamas Don't Let Your Babies Grow Up to Be Cowboys."

The next year, 1979, his songs and performance skills brought him both CMA's Entertainer of the Year award and the Academy of Country Music's (ACM) Entertainer of the Year award.

Willie had definitely climbed his musical mountains by 1979, but he still had other lofty barriers to scale.

As a youngster he had watched the cowboy movie heroes jump on their horses to chase away the bad guys and gain the everlasting gratitude of downtrodden farmers, threatened townsfolk, and damsels in distress.

He admits to fantasizing about himself as the hero of the romantic yarns of the Old West. Two cowboy stars were his favorites. Roy Rogers and Gene Autry were singing cowboys, and when they finished the chases and stopped the villains, they got off their horses to pick and sing. Everyone in the movies seemed to appreciate their singing as much as their derring-do.

In other words, Willie had a secret ambition to act. And like his boyhood heroes, he thought he wouldn't mind singing in Western movies.

Hollywood had also taken notice, as his songs skyrocketed up the charts. Music was a big part of the movies in the seventies, and Willie's music took him to California frequently. On one such occasion, Robert Redford asked him if he would like to be in an upcoming film.

The movie was *Electric Horseman*, released in 1979. Once more the boy from Abbott, Texas, proved that just about anything is possible in America. Willie launched his acting career, without any training whatsoever, at the tender age of forty-six. Again, he found a new beginning at an age when many in that field would have seen their careers ending.

"I was really worried . . . whether he was going to be able to handle it or not," says producer Sidney Pollack. "He had a real odd aptitude immediately, like he has in his singing . . . a kind of honesty."

Willie did get a chance to sing in his first Western movie, even though it was a far cry from the romantic oaters that inspired him as a boy. In one drinking scene, he and Redford sing it up off-key in a sleazy motel room.

In another scene, Willie ad-libbed, "I don't know what *you're* gonna do. I'm gonna get me a bottle of tequila and one of those little Keno girls who can suck the chrome off a trailer hitch and kinda kick back." So naturally did Willie take to acting that the ad-lib stayed in the final cut.

"I always felt that acting was like conversation," Willie admits. "I always felt life and the movies had to be pretty much alike."

He played the role of a manager to Redford's rodeo cowboy and believes the role was natural for him. In other words, it was Willie playing Willie.

"Playing Robert Redford's manager, that didn't require a lot of stretch. Rambo, however, is another deal, or Mozart might have been a little hard for me," he quips.

Although *Electric Horseman* was his first feature film, Nelson was not a complete stranger to the film medium. *Austin City Limits*, the weekly music special produced in Austin and aired nationwide on the Public Broadcasting System (PBS), was inaugurated

THROUGH HIS MUSIC AND HIS INTRODUCTION TO THE BROAD GENERAL PUBLIC IN HIS MOVIE ROLES ON THE BIG SCREEN, WILLIE HAD GROWN FROM OBSCURE COUNTRY SINGER TO A NATIONAL POP ICON.

in 1976. Willie was among the first entertainers showcased. Inspired by Austin's burgeoning music scene of that era, Willie was instrumental in getting the show off the ground.

The format was perfect for Nelson because of his interest in bringing diverse musical cultures together. *Austin City Limits*, while heavily country, also features blues and bluegrass, folk and zydeco. Willie, with his own eclectic style, fit into the format well. Willie actually taped the pilot performance for *Austin City Limits* in 1974, two years before the program became a regular feature on PBS, with thirteen new shows a year.

Although at the time the pilot was produced Willie was not yet well known outside his small core of fans, in 1975, his show set fund-raising records for PBS stations across the South, where it was viewed before its release to the rest of the country. His film presence and

WILLIE, THE OUTLAW SINGER
WHO HAD BROKEN DOWN MUSICAL BARRIERS, WAS
A MOVIE ACTOR
IN HIS OWN RIGHT. HE WOULD GO ON
TO APPEAR IN THIRTY-ONE
BIG-SCREEN FILMS
MADE-FOR-TV MOVIES, AND
FILM DOCUMENTARIES
OVER THE NEXT TWO DECADES

personal magnetism were obvious, even in this early film effort. His appearance in that pilot, which was primarily a funding project, resulted in PBS ordering ten more programs for 1976, and *Austin City Limits* was launched.

Nelson was certainly not the stereotypical movie star in appearance, manner, or acting talent. His small role in his first movie, however, convinced Hollywood that he had something the audience would respond to. His forthright delivery of the ad-lib about the chrome trailer hitch in *Electric Horseman* drew the loudest laughs from the audiences of that tragi-comedy, and those lines were quoted or misquoted broadly for years. Willie told *Texas Monthly* magazine that the lines were loosely derived from a novel written by two of his Texas friends, Bud Shrake and Dan Jenkins, former Dallas newspapermen.

Willie was back in Hollywood for his second feature movie the following year, when he made *Honeysuckle Rose*. In that film, he plays a music-maker who almost loses his wife because of the demands of the road. The storyline could be considered too close for comfort to a musician with Willie's own marital problems.

He wrote the classic traveling song "On the Road Again" for *Honeysuckle Rose*. Willie modestly recalls how that song was "whipped out" for the film:

"They said, 'We need some music for the movie and we'd like to have a sort of theme song.' I said, 'Okay, what do you want it to say?' They said, 'Something about being on the road.'"

Sidney Pollack, the film's producer, completes the story:

"Willie's sitting there and he says in kind of a monotone: 'On the road again . . . I just can't wait to get on the road again . . . and the life I love is making music with my friends . . . I just can't wait to get on the road again.'"

Willie turned to Pollack and asked, "What do you think?"

"I said, 'Boy, I don't know. What about the music?' And he said, 'Don't worry about that. I'll get the music.'"

Sure enough, in a few days "On the Road Again" was ready as the theme for the movie and went on to become a major and enduring hit for Willie. It was the top song on the *Music from Honeysuckle Rose* album.

Through his music and his introduction to the broad general public in his movie roles on the big screen, Willie had grown from an

obscure country singer to a national icon. The roguish, smiling outlaw lifestyle he represented caught on with the mood of America's young people, and the redheaded stranger became a sort of living folk hero—a modern day Robin Hood figure.

Willie, the outlaw singer who had broken down musical barriers, was a movie actor in his own right. He would go on to appear in thirty-one big-screen films, made-for-TV movies, and film documentaries over the next two decades.

Some of the films gained wide recognition, in part because of the unique characterization he could bring to projects. In most cases Willie was portraying Willie, or characters very much like the real person.

Among his big-screen film credits are *Thief* (1981), *Barbarosa* (1982), *Songwriter* (1984), *Walking After Midnight* (1988), *Big Country* (1994), *Dust to Dust* (1994), *Starlight* (1996), *Gone Fishin'* (1997), and *Half Baked* (1998). He appeared in the controversial *Wag the Dog*, which by uncanny timing became embroiled in the controversies of the Clinton presidential impeachment in 1997.

In addition to his impressive list of big-screen movie credits, Willie landed

significant roles in as many made-for-TV movies. His first television-movie appearance was *In the Jailhouse Now* (1982); a second TV film, *Coming Out of the Ice*, appeared the same year. One of his biggest TV roles was in *Stagecoach* (1986). Another credit that year included *The Last Days of Frank and Jesse James*. In 1988, he appeared in three TV movies: *Baja Oklahoma*, *Dynamite and Gold*, and *Once Upon a Texas Train*.

In 1995, he did tribute to another country music icon when he acted in the television rendition of the Dottie West story, *Big Dreams and Broken Hearts*.

The film role that brought him closest to personal stardom came in 1986, with the movie that many said was a thinly veiled insight into another side of Willie. That movie was *Red Headed Stranger*.

In *Red Headed Stranger*, Willie stars as a Western preacher who turns outlaw and sinks into depravity after finding his wife—played by Morgan Fairchild—in the arms of a lover. The preacher shoots the unfaithful pair, but later rises to the occasion to save himself and the whole town from the bad guys.

While many of his associates and fans knew Willie was raised, and first sang, in the

WHEN HE DECIDES THAT A PROJECT OR A CAUSE IS WORTHWHILE—WHETHER IN HIS CAREER OR HIS PERSONAL LIFE—HE SELDOM LETS GO UNTIL IT IS COMPLETED.

strongly fundamentalist Protestant churches of his childhood, few people are aware of his deeply held spiritual beliefs. Fewer still know that he was named to the board of directors of a theological seminary some years ago.

There is a small church located on one of Willie's Texas Hill Country properties, which was used in one of his movies. Willie, family members, and friends from the community often worship there on Sundays. His daughter Lana regularly brings a dozen or so people out to the place for prayer, singing, and discussions.

"Red Headed Stranger" was an old song that had been around for years. Willie often sang it to his children at bedtime, and it meant a lot to him personally. When he began writing the songs for the album with that title, he believed the theme would make a great movie.

"I'd always thought that, ever since I heard the song," Willie says. "I knew this would be a movie. It's already a movie in music."

Two years after the album and the "Blue Eyes" single from it made such a hit, Willie resurrected the idea for the movie. He approached scriptwriter Bill Wittliff with the concept, and the project was underway. But it would take years more before the movie was released.

Willie invested his own money in building a small Old West town on his Pedernales River property to be the scene for this movie and other film projects in the future. The little town had the church at one end and a bordello at the other, with a saloon in the middle.

"So we have the good and the bad represented," Willie grins.

From concept to release, the movie *Red Headed Stranger* took twelve years. This project could well be a metaphor for Willie's tenacious approach to life. When he decides that a project or a cause is worthwhile—whether in his career or his personal life—he seldom lets go until it is completed. ★

FARM AID WAS BORN, WITH THE SLOGAN: *KEEP AMERICA GROWING!*

Willie's exposure to movie stardom did not change the man or his focus. Between every filmmaking stint he always returned to his first love—his music. And he never forgot during those heady years that the most important thing about his music was his audience.

"On the Road Again," the theme song from Honeysuckle Rose, became a favorite opener at his live appearances. It wasn't long before the tune became his own unofficial theme song, and it could not have been more appropriate.

If he had settled down in his new home in the foothills and low mountains west of Austin, it was only to establish a base for his travels and a permanent home for his children. He and Connie now had two daughters, Paula and Amy. Willie also remained very close to his three children from his first marriage to Martha. Daughter Lana lived with her family at her father's original ranch near Dripping Springs and worked in his music enterprise. His sister, Bobbie, had been a part of his family band during these successful years; she, too, lived nearby. His ranch complex thirty miles east of Austin, in the Briarcliff area, provided housing for others in his troupe. He was surrounded by family.

Willie Nelson's life in the late 1970s and early eighties must have seemed like the American dream come true to most of his fans. He was immensely successful in the competitive entertainment industry. Connie, his adoring and beautiful blonde wife, shared his interest in music, often traveling with him when he was on the road. Their relationship had endured the challenges of his rapid rise from near obscurity to fame after they moved together to Texas from Nashville, shortly after their marriage in 1971.

When Willie wasn't immersed in his career, he and Connie might be found with their two daughters enjoying the relative privacy of a ranch they owned in Colorado. The ranchette, more like a mountain retreat, was high in the Rocky Mountains, out of Evergreen. Situated on 116 scenic acres, the property featured a 4,700-square-foot main lodge, two guest houses, a caretaker's house, and stables.

A glimpse into the good life Willie and Connie shared was captured in a picture taken and later published by well-known photographer and photojournalist Harry Benson. The picture—which appeared in a photo book of celebrities including Ronald and Nancy Reagan, Queen Noor al-Hussein of Jordan, General Normal Schwarzkopf, Michael Jackson, and scores of other world-famous faces—showed a happily frolicking Willie, submerged in soap suds in a large red tub with his wife, Connie. The red tub was a fixture of that favorite mountain hideaway, where Willie and his family could relax together from the stress and strain of sudden success, and far removed from the busy demands of his ranch headquarters out of Austin.

But as the years went by, success in music and movies also made demands on the marriage. Willie and Connie's daughters, Paula and Amy, were reaching an age when school involvement was becoming important. Connie was finding it increasingly more difficult to get away and accompany Willie on concert tours and filming sessions. They had met at a concert in a small Texas town north of Houston on one of his road tours more than ten years before, and she had traveled with him extensively up to that time.

Now Willie was not only traveling more because of his moviemaking, but keeping up an exhaustive schedule of live performances, as well as a near-manic pace of writing and record production.

On the road again, Willie maintained a whirlwind schedule of personal appearances in concert halls, Las Vegas clubs, auditoriums, and even larger dance halls. But his live performances remained the most enjoyable of all his activities, because that was where he could be with his fans. In the decade after he moved his family to Austin, Nelson conducted an average of 250 personal performances each year.

In the five-year period from 1980 to 1985, Willie's output in records, movies, and live concerts was nothing short of incredible. He released sixty-seven albums in that brief period, including many of the songs that became all-time favorites with his legion of fans.

"On the Road Again" won him another Grammy in 1980 for Best Country Song. *Yesterday's Wine* was re-released to acclaim

IN THE FIVE-YEAR PERIOD FROM 1980 TO 1985, WILLIE'S OUTPUT IN RECORDS, MOVIES, AND LIVE CONCERTS WAS NOTHING SHORT OF INCREDIBLE. HE RELEASED SIXTY-SEVEN ALBUMS IN THAT BRIEF PERIOD, INCLUDING MANY OF THE SONGS THAT BECAME ALL-TIME FAVORITES WITH HIS LEGION OF FANS.

in 1980, and a dozen other albums were released in 1981.

Then in 1982, Willie made another classic hit that assured him a permanent place in the minds and hearts of longtime fans and newcomers to his music alike. Columbia Records released the album *Always on My Mind* that year, and Willie swept every honor that the industry could bestow. In 1982, "Always on My Mind" won CMA's Single of the Year and Album of the Year awards. The ACM also gave him double awards that year, for best single and best album. And to cap off his honors, he won the 1982 Grammy for the Best Country Vocal Performance by a male entertainer for "Always on My Mind."

All the sudden success led to a degree of fame and a level of fortune that the poor boy from Abbott, Texas, had never dreamed possible. In a few short years, Willie's earnings from hit albums, songwriting royalties, personal

OVER THE YEARS, FARM AID HAS GROWN FROM A GIANT CONCERT, TELEVISED COAST-TO-COAST, INTO A YEAR-ROUND MOVEMENT. JOINED BY JOHN MELLENCAMP AND NEIL YOUNG, WILLIE CONTINUES TO WORK ON THIS BENEFIT BY BRINGING IN HUNDREDS OF ENTERTAINERS WHO DONATE THEIR TIME, TALENT, AND MONEY TO GIVE SOMETHING BACK TO THE RURAL COMMUNITIES THAT RAISED MANY OF THEM

appearances, and movies made up for the long struggle to the top. Naturally, he had dreamed of a place for himself and his family all those years that he was dodging landlords for the rent and moving his family from one tiny house to another in the middle of the night.

He had enjoyed such a home at Ridgetop after his early successes in Nashville, and upon relocating to Texas to a place in the country with some acreage. But his skyrocketing fortune in the late 1970s and early eighties finally enabled him to surround himself with any environment he wanted. He did not choose a mansion among the stars in Hollywood, a Southern plantation, a gated estate, or a penthouse in a city. Instead, he chose the scenic, yet rugged, Hill Country west of Austin.

Willie found a 700-plus acre ranch, along with a defunct country club across the road, with greens stretching along a scenic river. The site was surrounded by the low foothills that drop off Texas's high Edwards Plateau. The springs from aquifers along the plateau's edge feed the Pedernales, Guadalupe, and Colorado Rivers, cutting through canyons carved from limestone. White rock outcroppings and cliffs, dotted with gnarled junipers and scrubby cedar, provide a landscape that could be right out of a classic Western movie.

The land where Willie settled is rich with the history of battles between Comanches and Texas Rangers, cattle barons and bandits. Willie could thrive in this environment, because he draws on a strong sense of the history and cul-ture of the Western frontier for his songs. Even his independent lifestyle reflects the attitudes of the Old West in many ways.

In his "neighborhood" there is more recent history, too. Willie's property is not far from the famous Pedernales River ranch of the late President Lyndon Baines Johnson and his historic family farm and birthplace.

The country remains wild and largely

undeveloped, despite the building of a string of big conservation dams a short hop north of Willie's ranch. The big reservoirs—Lake Buchanan, Lake Marble Falls, Lake LBJ, Lake Travis, and Lake Austin—provide year-round recreation for the citizens of Central Texas's booming high-tech metropolitan cities of Austin and San Antonio. But resort development on the lakes is far enough away to leave Willie with the natural privacy and space that inspires his song-making.

This is horse country, and Willie was able to keep a stable of horses for his frequent use, and for the pleasure of visitors and the host of family members and friends who settled around the property.

In addition to the country club, the land had a few outbuildings and houses already established on it. There was plenty of room for his extended family to take up residences nearby.

The golf course on the property he bought was part of the former Pedernales Country Club, and now Willie had his own private fairways and greens. His favorite recreational activity had long been golf, and so this bonus property included in the purchase was just fine with him. He once told friends that his ambition was to retire young and work as a deejay so he could play golf as much as he wanted. However, approaching the age, and with the financial means to enjoy such an ambition, retirement was nowhere in sight. But he did take advantage of the golf course, which he decided to keep open and in playing shape.

The 5,000-square-foot home he built was described in an article in *Country Music* magazine as a rather strange, lodgelike dwelling: "basically one giant room." There were no walls to separate the living, working, sleeping, eating, and kitchen areas. The magazine article described a bathroom in the home as being "the size of a restaurant."

The small Western town he built on the property as a movie prop for *Red Headed Stranger* fit naturally into the surrounding countryside, because it was a replica of the legendary little towns that had dotted this same Texas frontier a century earlier. Friends talk about the eerie pleasure of riding horses with Willie through the streets of an authentic, well-maintained, but empty frontier town, and the feeling of stepping back into the Old West that such an experience generates.

As ideal as this cherished retreat might have been for Willie and his family, the demands of his mushrooming career kept him away from home far more than he or his family might have wished. There was plenty of room on the new property to conceal from view his big over-the-road touring caravan, which included the *Honeysuckle Rose*, two other buses for his band and tour company, and an equipment truck. In

those years of constant travel, Willie often spent as much time aboard the *Honeysuckle Rose* as he did on his new Texas spread. His personal bus, a traveling office, was outfitted with beds, showers, TV and stereo sets, and kitchen facilities. The rolling headquarters offered all the comforts a home-away-from-home could pack, and it was Willie's pride and joy.

But "home" was back on the ranch, which writer and longtime friend Gary Cartwright of *Texas Monthly* magazine called "Willie World" in a cover feature on Nelson in 1998. And that description is probably more accurate than intended, because it was here that Willie Nelson was able to create the world as he believed it should be.

He had also realized one of his oldest dreams. He was able to have his own recording studio on his property. From this state-of-the-art studio, surrounded by a place that any old cowboy would swear was heaven, Willie was able to create the incredible number of songs and recordings flowing forth in this music-rich five years of his life.

After a string of platinum records resulting from music written for the films he acted in, Willie's albums went on to capture top billing on the charts in an endless train that seemed would go on forever. He not only made many

solo hits but during this prolific period tried several new styles of music and duet performances with singers from other musical genres. And he still made albums with his old friends from earlier times, including Waylon and Kris.

Many of Nelson's song titles, sprinkled through albums produced by RCA, Columbia, Delta, and a half-dozen smaller labels, are forever lodged in the annals of America's music history.

He also continued to receive the adulation of his peers, winning a CMA Best Vocal Male Duo award in 1983 with Merle Haggard.

His influence now reached far beyond the country music field. In 1983, he received one of the most unique awards of his career. The National Academy of Popular Music gave him its Lifetime Achievement award. Willie Nelson was the first country artist ever honored with this distinguished recognition, and only the fourth recipient in the Academy's history.

The awards kept rolling in almost as fast as Willie could turn out new albums. He shared the CMA's Best Vocal Duo of the Year in 1984 with Julio Iglesias for "To All the Girls I've Loved Before." It was another award of many for Willie, but clearly a surprise first country music honor for the popular Latin singer. The ACM also gave

its 1984 Single of the Year to Willie and Julio for the song.

Nelson and Kris Kristofferson shared another coveted ACM award in 1984. They were presented the Tex Ritter award for outstanding achievement as songwriters. And to round out the 1984 recognitions, in a tribute that once again proved Willie's wide-ranging talents, he shared ACM's 1984 Top Single Record award with Johnny Cash, Waylon Jennings, and Kristofferson for "The Highwayman."

The saying "He's generous to a fault" could have been coined for Willie Nelson.

Anyone who knew anything about Nelson over the years was aware that he was a sharing man who helped out family, old friends and new, and sometimes strangers in need of a hand up. He had been down plenty of times himself. Even in the past he had often stretched his own thin income to help out when he could barely help himself or his growing family. His newly acquired wealth only made it easier for Willie to help others.

Everyone around him admits that Willie knew very little about his own sudden wealth, entrusting his finances to a cadre of promoters, accountants, and advisors. And if he knew little about the financial side of his growing empire, he couldn't have seemed to care less, often

saying it only gave him the wherewithal to do his music the way he knew it should be done.

"He wants to take care of everyone. His family and everyone else in the world," sister Bobbie says. "He would, too, if he could."

Willie admits that he has a soft spot for the underdog and the downtrodden.

"Whenever anyone sees an injustice being done they have to decide either to do something or do nothing," he says. "Since I'm basically a troublemaker, I like to jump into things and see 'what's going on here' and how I can help, what I can do."

At this peak in his career, Willie saw a major injustice going on all over America, and especially affecting a large segment of his loyal audience. American farmers and their families were suffering in almost unnoticed silence.

By 1985, family farms were being obliterated by the tens of thousands. Farm commodity prices were so low that farmers could no longer pay back their loans. Farmland values soared, as big corporations gobbled up rural real estate as fast as they could force lending institutions to foreclose on family farms. In less than one generation, from the early 1960s, farm population declined by two-thirds in the Great Breadbasket of the plains states.

Willie had a "sweat of the brow" kinship

WILLIE SEEMS EMBARRASSED, ALMOST APOLOGETIC WHEN ANYONE TRIES TO PRAISE HIM FOR THIS GIANT PHILANTHROPY. "ONCE YOU SEE HOW APPRECIATIVE THE FARMERS ARE WHEN ANYONE DOES ANYTHING TO HELP THEM, YOU CAN'T NOT DO IT," WILLIE SAYS.

with this rural population. His own childhood was spent living in poverty in a farm community. Whenever he was on tour, he witnessed firsthand the scenes of the farmers' demise: overalls-clad men, young and old, standing on ramshackle farmhouse porches, watching agents in white shirt and tie auctioning off their lives and livelihoods. Willie was deeply affected.

He was much too busy at this time in his life to take on anything else, but he was determined to do something beyond simply whipping out a personal check to ease his conscience.

"I was watching a TV show called *Live Aid*, and I heard Bob Dylan say, 'Wouldn't it be nice if some of that money stayed here in this country for our farmers?'" Willie recalls.

The solution hit him. Why not something similar to the international famine aid benefit, but staged primarily by country musicians in America's heartland for American farm families?

Farm Aid was born, with the slogan: *Keep America Growing!* Willie was on the phone immediately calling his outlaw friends and their outrider music contacts.

"Willie is one of those guys who doesn't ask for things frivolously," says Kenny Rogers about the call he received from Willie. "When he asks for something you know it's important."

On September 22, 1985, Willie stood on a stage in the pouring rain to launch a phenomenal benefit that has been repeated for a decade and a half and raised millions of dollars for farm families.

He opened the musical extravaganza with the shout that has echoed through the farm belt ever since: "Welcome to Farm Aid, the concert for America!"

Over the years, Farm Aid has grown from a giant concert, televised coast-to-coast, into a year-round movement. Joined by John Mellencamp and Neil Young, Willie continues to work on this benefit by bringing in hundreds of entertainers who donate their time, talent, and money to give something back to the rural communities that raised many of them.

The goal of the program is to provide assistance, in direct grants or low-interest loans, to keep farm families on their farms. Since 1985, a vast network of local organizations in forty-four states—coordinated by Farm Aid and including small-town and rural churches and social service agencies—has directed tens of millions into meeting that goal. Farm Aid has set up a national hotline that farm families can call when the going gets too rough for them to cope. The organizations provide emergency food, financial and emotional counseling, and other long- and short-term support services.

In 1997, the *Chicago Sun-Times* called the event a "feast of musical adventure." The benefit concerts have become as much a part of the American scene as apple pie. And, as singers for the Farm Aid concerts like to point out: "There would be no apples for that pie without America's farmers."

The shows are a musical smorgasbord, featuring bluegrass, country, rock 'n' roll, pop, Tejano, and Latino, and just about anything else a volunteering musician wishes to perform.

Among the artists who have donated time and performances are: Paul Simon, Bonnie Raitt, Lyle Lovett, Bryan Adams, Dwight Yoakam, Don Henley, Bruce Hornsby, Mary-Chapin Carpenter, the Grateful Dead, Tom Petty, the Neville Brothers, Hootie & the Blowfish, Bob Dylan, Kenny Rogers, the Dave Matthews Band, Tim McGraw, Jewel, the Allman Brothers Band, Martina McBride, and most of Willie's own musical sidekicks from his outlaw bunch. John Fogerty made his debut-solo appearance at one of the shows after leaving Creedence Clearwater Revival. Elton John reworked his

now famous "Candle in the Wind" for a special presentation at the 1997 Farm Aid concert, and Nelson himself added some reggae to his repertoire that year.

The crowds, averaging about 30,000 in attendance, in addition to the huge television audiences, are as much a mix as Willie's Fourth of July crowds—including everything from businessmen to bikers, along with his usual following of fans from rednecks to professors.

The concerts, which usually run for twelve hours, are heartland events and have been held at Champaign (Illinois), Austin, Lincoln, Indianapolis, Irving (Texas), Ames (Iowa), New Orleans, Louisville, Columbia (South Carolina), and Chicago.

The concerts themselves have raised more than $15 million in direct farm aid, in addition to an array of fund-raising and matching-fund activities encouraged by the Farm Aid organization.

"Willie just called me up and said, 'Hey I'm concerned about the farm issue in the U.S., and I guess you are, too,'" Farm Aid co-founder Mellencamp recalls. "He said, 'I'm gonna do something about it. Would you like to be a part of this?'"

Willie personally devotes many hours each year to making sure the show is a fund-raising success. Several years ago, when poor advance-ticket sales caused the show to be canceled in Dallas, Willie hustled around behind the scenes. Within two days he had found a new promoter in Chicago and moved the show. It sold out a few days later and the show went on to be one of the most successful fund-raisers in the history of the Farm Aid movement.

Willie seems embarrassed, almost apologetic when anyone tries to praise him for this giant philanthropy.

"Once you see how appreciative the farmers are when anyone does anything to help them, you can't not do it," Willie says.

Without expecting or asking for a favor in return, his openhearted contribution to the welfare of the American farmers was to be remembered in a very personal way in the not-too-distant future.

But at the time of the first Farm Aid benefit concert in 1985, the redheaded stranger was on the top of his mountain, and there was nothing but blue skies down his road as far as anyone could see. ★

SUCCESS DID NOT SEEM TO CHANGE THE MAN VISIBLY.

Willie was living in the promised land, and that was the theme song for an album with a similar name. The Promiseland was released in 1986 by Columbia.

His fantastic accomplishments, both in music and film, provided Willie and his family the means to enjoy an almost idyllic existence. At home in Austin, now in his fifties, Willie Nelson was the undisputed dean of the growing cadre of Texas-based musicians who flocked to Austin's increasingly important music scene.

A millionaire several times over, he seemed to have settled down to enjoy a serene family life. He and his wife, Connie, made a home for their two young daughters; and Willie's three older children, now grown and independent, stayed in close touch.

Despite his life on the road, Willie was now very much the head of an extended family himself. It had been a long, often grueling rise to the top, since the days when the preteen Willie had been forced to assume so much family responsibility after the sudden death of his grandfather.

Willie had taken his son, Billy, who was born in 1958, to live at his Ridgetop, Tennessee, home soon after his separation from his first wife, Martha. When Willie moved to Austin, he took his son along, to raise in Texas. Susie, Willie's younger daughter from that marriage, had also come to live with her father. Lana, with children of her own, moved to Austin soon after Willie relocated there, and the family had been together ever since.

Billy struggled to build his own career in country music. He had been a stand-in for country music singer Merle Haggard during the filming of the music video *Pancho and Lefty* in 1983, and had also recorded a country gospel record of his own.

The musical family, including Willie's sister, Bobbie, often surprised Austin fans by showing up unannounced at a Western music club or event. They readily accepted invitations from the audience to take the stage for impromptu and unpaid performances. On such occasions Billy and his famous dad would thrill an audience with a song or two, or sometimes a whole set.

After reaching young adulthood, Billy left Texas and returned to the Nashville area to try to make it on his own. He married and settled down outside of the country music capital. Whenever Willie was in Nashville, he and the son he had raised in the world of country music would be together.

Back in Texas, the growing Nelson clan was joined at Willie's headquarters west of Austin by an extended, adopted family that not only included distant blood relatives but loyal employees who had been with Willie for years.

"He was happy," Lana says of that time in Willie's life.

Success did not seem to change the man visibly. Locals were often surprised to see a man with a familiar face walking unescorted through the airport or in shops around town. Occasionally, the time-weathered face might cause a double-take, and if it did the gawker got a friendly nod and wink.

"That guy looked exactly like Willie Nelson," a surprised airport visitor might say.

"It was," the local would answer nonchalantly.

His adopted city had dramatically prospered and changed, too. Austin's population had almost doubled, from about 225,000 in the early 1970s when Willie moved there from Nashville, to nearly 500,000 by the mid-1980s. Suddenly computer-technology plants began springing up everywhere in the pasture land around the city. Lockheed Aerospace, IBM, Motorola, 3M Corporation, and the home-grown infant, Dell Corporation, all built sprawling, high-tech facilities in Austin during the eighties. While most of this business boom was attributed to the introduction of high technology into the area's economy, music also

WILLIE WAS ON TOP OF THE WORLD AGAIN AS THE DECADE CAME TO A CLOSE. BUT HE DIDN'T CHOOSE TO REST ON HIS LAURELS. HIS SCHEDULE, WHICH MIGHT HAVE KILLED A MUCH YOUNGER PERFORMER, SEEMED TO INVIGORATE HIM.

played an important role in the new prosperity.

Willie's successful music and film operations, centered at his ranch west of Austin, encouraged all types of creative film and musical innovations. Scores of clubs offering live music flourished in the Austin area. One entire downtown street—Sixth Street—was dedicated to live music.

This activity led to the establishment of the annual South by Southwest music festival. The success of that event led the "little city" of Austin to lay claim to the title "Live Music Capital of the World." Every March, South by Southwest draws crowds of music and film lovers, performers, and critics from around the world for a two-week music and film extravaganza.

The demands of career were taking a heavy toll on Willie's time. During this period he rarely slowed down, going from movie to concert to benefit to nightclub performance to recording studio. He may have begun to realize that there was something more to life

than the glitz of the entertainment life. In 1986, he and his sister recorded the spiritual album *I'd Rather Have Jesus*.

Willie was on top of the world again as the decade came to a close. But he didn't choose to rest on his laurels. His schedule, which might have worn out a much younger performer, seemed to invigorate him.

In addition to his longtime "musical outlaw" comrades—Kristofferson, Jennings, and Johnny Cash, who with Willie made up the Highwaymen—Willie reached beyond the country music fold to perform with stars from other fields of music. He recorded duets with singers from such diverse musical backgrounds as Julio Iglesias, Bob Dylan, Ray Charles, Leon Russell, Dolly Parton, and Neil Young.

Nineteen eighty-six was also a very active moviemaking year for Willie. He performed in the television movies *Stagecoach* and *Last Days of Frank and Jesse James*. That was also the year the biggest personal movie of his career, *Red Headed Stranger*, was filmed, largely at his own ranch.

Several of his old albums were reissued and a number of his best songs were combined into new albums. He had several new albums issued, too, *Seashores of Old Mexico* and *A Horse Called Music*. Simon and Schuster published the story of Willie's life, *Willie: An Autobiography*, which he wrote with Texas author Bud Shrake, in 1988.

Despite all of the record and movie releases in the 1980s, Willie seemed driven to maintain personal contact with his fans. He never slacked off on a killing performance schedule. However, now there was a troubling difference in meeting this demanding schedule. His vivacious blonde wife, Connie, was less able to accompany him in his travels, because their daughters were now school-age and could not make the trips. Connie stayed home with the kids, and Willie went on the road with his crew. As in the past, the long periods of absence began to place strains on his sixteen-year marriage.

By 1986, at the height of his fame and success, the hazards of the road were catching

SUDDENLY THE T-MEN HIT HIM WITH A TAX BILL FOR MORE THAN TWO MILLION DOLLARS, CLAIMING HE OWED TAXES FROM CONCERTS, ROYALTIES, MUSIC PUBLISHING, AND FAN-CLUB SOUVENIRS.

up with him. Connie and Willie separated and in 1989, they were divorced.

"I can't go around feeling guilty about doing something that I felt I was put here to do," Willie laments. "I feel good about doing it [live performances]—it's what I've always done, it's probably what I will always do. And people around me, they either accept me that way or they don't."

In 1989, Columbia released a new version of the album *On the Road Again*, and *Highwayman II* was released at the end of the year.

Everyone in the industry figured Willie Nelson had done just about all there was to do. He was fifty-six years old, and the red beard and braids were beginning to show a lot of gray.

At the last musical-award shows of the decade, Willie was still winning top honors. But to some of his peers, these awards may have seemed like final tributes to a career drawing to a close. The National Academy of Recording Arts & Sciences awarded Willie the 1989 Grammy for Lifetime Achievement. A few minutes later there was yet another honor for his years of contributions to American music. The Academy gave a special Grammy to Willie called a "Living Legend Award."

While Willie was appropriately appreciative, as he usually was in his humble way, he had absolutely no intention of hanging up his guitar and bandanna. Nelson was not about to rest on his laurels.

As the 1980s drew to a close, storm clouds were beginning to blot out the blue skies that had graced Willie's recent life.

He worked on a new album, entitled *Born for Trouble*, to launch the decade of the 1990s. Ominously, the title could have foretold what was just ahead for Willie Hugh Nelson in the next few months.

Willie was a phenomenal songwriter, singer, guitarist, and entertainer. Few would argue that he was, and is, a musical genius. As such, he did not care much about the business side, just so long as his family and friends and those employees dependent on his continued success were taken care of, while he had the freedom to ply his talent in his own way.

Although he eschewed the day-to-day bean-counting, he was not irresponsible when it came to financial matters. Nelson had sought out what he thought to be the best financial, accounting, and legal advice he could buy, to keep straight the complex money flow from myriad sources. He employed experts from highly recommended professional services to manage his affairs and handle the books for the tax people.

The first sign that there might be a serious problem, beyond what entertainers often seem to have with the Internal Revenue Service, came in early 1986. Suddenly the T-men hit him with a tax bill for more than two million dollars, claiming he owed taxes from concerts, royalties, music publishing, and fan-club souvenirs. In addition, the government filed

WILLIE WAS A PHENOMENAL SONGWRITER
SINGER, GUITARIST, AND ENTERTAINER
FEW WOULD ARGUE
THAT HE WAS, AND IS, A MUSICAL GENIUS
AS SUCH, HE DID NOT CARE MUCH
ABOUT THE BUSINESS SIDE
JUST SO LONG AS HIS FAMILY AND FRIENDS
AND THOSE EMPLOYEES DEPENDENT ON HIS
CONTINUED SUCCESS
WERE TAKEN CARE OF, WHILE HE HAD FREEDOM TO PLY HIS
TALENT IN HIS OWN WAY

IN NUMEROUS CASES, AFTER HEARING HARD-LUCK STORIES, HE WOULD CONCLUDE THE CONVERSATION WITH, "CAN A LITTLE MONEY HELP?" WILLIE OFTEN WHIPPED OUT HIS CHECKBOOK AND WROTE THE PETITIONERS A GENEROUS PERSONAL CHECK.

claims for another half-million dollars against his Willie Nelson Music Company.

His accountants and lawyers had worked out minor tax problems in the past and, at first, this looked like more of the same. However, now the government was not just demanding payment for taxes and penalties, it also claimed he had taken improper deductions and evaded taxes "fraudulently with intent." A special tax-court trial judge was named to his case, and Willie was facing some serious late charges and penalties.

All Willie was worried about was "proving to them that I was not a criminal and I wasn't trying to evade my taxes."

Nelson's lawyers said these allegations were "absolutely groundless" and charged that the government was giving the false impression that the now-famous singer had violated federal laws by evading taxes.

"I didn't have two million in my pocket at the time," says Willie. "So rather than go borrow two million dollars, my lawyers and accountants decided that what I should do is borrow *twelve* million dollars and get into a cattle-feeding deal."

The IRS had disallowed business expense and investment losses that Willie's tax managers had claimed over several years.

The big plan for windfall tax deductions, cobbled together by the best tax advice from his silk-stocking consultants, only made matters worse. The livestock-feeder investments crashed as well. By the time the dispute with the IRS came to a head, Willie's two million dollar debt was a thing of the past. The government now claimed he owed a whopping $32 million in taxes.

"After a while it got kind of funny, because here I am—a guitar player from Abbott, Texas—owing these guys thirty million dollars," he jokes about the outrageous size of the alleged debt.

But in the back of his mind Willie came to the realization that something was very wrong. "How could they let that happen?" he wondered. "Someone was not watching the store."

It could happen because, for Willie, money never was the motivation. It had always been about the music.

When the tax complaints against Willie became public knowledge, and it appeared there was a good possibility that country music's biggest star was in serious financial trouble, the news media had a field day. One screaming headline in a national tabloid read: "Willie Nelson Homeless and Broke!"

It was not long before reporters were digging deep into the very private affairs of the famous star.

One of *Texas Monthly*'s top investigative reporters, Robert Draper, dug the deepest.

Instead of finding the usual seamy story of a sex-and-drugs indulgent life of a superstar, the cover story revealed something that was almost as embarrassing to the quiet, unpretentious Willie.

Contrary to the legend of an outlaw raging on the wild side of life, what Draper's investigation and subsequent cover story revealed was an unassuming, generous, good neighbor who collected stray people like some eccentrics pick up stray cats. Willie's spacious Hill Country ranch was dotted with small homes he had provided, free of rent, to a menagerie of down-and-outers. Some of Willie's beneficiaries had been provided jobs, too. Others were legitimate workers in his musical enterprise. An aged pauper was comfortably ensconced in a cabin by the river as a sort of game warden, with free rent but no apparent duties.

Draper also found case after case of Willie's largesse spread among staff members and their families, and even strangers. In addition to his well-known philanthropies such as Farm Aid, the redheaded stranger had donated time and talent to more than one hundred benefit performances for various causes over a two-year period.

The magazine writer also uncovered stories of Willie's personal charity toward his fans. It was revealed that following many of his appearances, when Willie was noted for going out and spending hours talking with fans, he was handing out more than autographs. Word had spread that "Willie will help out." In numerous cases, after hearing hard-luck stories, he would conclude the conversation with, "Can a little money help?" Willie often whipped out his checkbook and wrote the petitioners a generous personal check.

Only a few members of Willie's closest family knew what he had been doing for years. His daughter Lana philosophically believed it was her daddy's business to do with his money whatever made him happy. She estimated that he probably never saw more than 10 percent of what he earned.

Willie got into financial trouble, too, because he was trusting of others. That faith in human nature was instilled in him as a child growing up in the tight-knit little prairie town where everyone helped everyone else.

The way Willie was raised, contracts were concluded with a simple nod and a handshake. He still conducted himself pretty much the same way, even though now Willie was playing for high stakes in the dog-eat-dog business world. He wasn't about to change at this stage in his life.

"He's very trusting," daughter Lana says. If someone in his loyal entourage, a family member, or an employee, questioned that a deal might not be good for him or on the up-and-up, Willie would shrug and reply, "Well, yeah, but you know in the long run, I think it's going to be worth it."

Lana, who tried to help Willie with his business at the time, says that occasionally someone would out-and-out lie to her dad. But "in the long run, I think that even the poor decisions worked out."

Of course, one of the problems with Willie's kind of personal, private, and undocumented charities was that the IRS was not impressed. If Willie had given away a lot of his fortune, the government maintained he should have done so after he paid his taxes.

Willie had been assured that the tax shelters he had been put into were legit, and that no taxes were due. But by the time the tax case was brought against him, there wasn't even enough cash to pay off a greatly reduced settlement offer made by the IRS.

Willie learned that the IRS was looking seriously at confiscating everything he owned, including his beat-up old guitar.

Willie ended the dynamic decade faced with losing everything he had struggled to build since leaving Abbott, Texas, as a broke teenager in the 1950s. Yet he was not a beaten man.

He worried more about protecting that battered old guitar from the IRS than about the loss of his properties in Colorado, Hawaii, and several Southern states. He was also worried about what might become of the extended family now dependent on him, not only for their livelihoods but literally for their homes located around his sprawling Hill Country properties.

Regarding the rest of his fortune, he had made it before. He told everyone that all he needed was his guitar named "Trigger." He was referring to the battered six-string Martin—the same instrument that he'd waded into the smoking ruins of his Nashville farm to save twenty years earlier.

There seemed to be something magical, almost alive, in that instrument, at least in the effect it had on Willie. With all his acquired wealth he had never opted to replace it with a finer instrument. The guitar, which had been with him since the very beginning, was as road-battered as Willie himself. It had been hocked during the bad times and redeemed from the pawn shop with each new royalty or honky-tonk job.

The instrument has been used for so long that it sports an extra hole worn by his fingers beneath the strings by decades of strumming. Willie attributes the unique sounds he can force from the guitar to that extra hole.

As the last decade of the twentieth century began, it appeared very possible that Willie Hugh Nelson was facing the loss of everything he had worked for. Literally nearing the age when most men are preparing to retire, he was starting over, with just that old wooden and wire tool of his trade.

Oddly, he seemed undaunted by the prospect.

"As long as I've got my guitar, I'll be fine," he told the *Texas Monthly* writer Draper for the cover feature entitled "Poor Willie." ★

JUST BECAUSE HE COULDN'T WORK DID NOT MEAN HE WASN'T BUSY.

Willie's world came crashing down as the new decade began. *The IRS rolled up to his spacious cabin with tax liens on everything he had spent a lifetime building.*

Government agents stormed into his offices and recording studio at the seventy-six-acre Pedernales Country Club property. They demanded of the startled employees that they open hidden vaults, which did not exist, and turn over secret files and ledger books, which also did not exist. Musical instruments, recording equipment, and all the tools that would have enabled Willie to continue to work were confiscated.

They moved on to his 5,000-square-foot home, impounding platinum albums, posters, and movie mementos—memorabilia from a lifetime. They stormed the home of his daughter Lana, where she lived with her children on the forty-four-acre Dripping Springs ranch that Willie had built when he first moved to Austin. Across the country, agents were taking custody of twenty other properties in four states.

"They just came in and said, 'We're with the IRS and you can take your purse and go,'" Lana remembers of that dark day in 1990. "They seized everything he had. They put locks on all the doors, all the buildings, all the houses."

Willie was in Hawaii at the time of the IRS foreclosure raids and had his guitar Trigger with him. Otherwise, this prized possession and vital tool of his trade would have been confiscated, too.

After the government sweep, Willie was left standing alone, almost like the young man who had walked off the farm in Abbott, some forty years earlier. Again, it was Willie and a beat-up old guitar against the world. This time, however, his future prospects seemed even more grim. His income from royalties and personal appearances, while still substantial, had been steadily declining since the mid-1980s. And now there were a lot more people depending on him, not the least of which was his new young family.

After Connie divorced him, Willie had married Anne-Marie D'Angelo, a makeup artist he met on one of the movie sets. He and Anne-Marie had two toddlers, Lukas and Jacob, living with them at Willie's Hill Country home at the time of the foreclosure. Then there was the well-being of other members of his extended family, and his score of employees to consider, too.

Willie knew he had assumed big responsibilities and that he did not have the luxury to give up, which just about anyone would have been tempted to do, with a $32 million tax debt filed against him. He felt the amount the government claimed was "way wrong." It was largely interest and penalties on taxes he disputed owing in the first place.

Regardless, of his protests, the IRS had the right to seize everything.

"He could have taken the easy way out and declared bankruptcy. He would have had to go back on promises made to other people and he wasn't going to do that. I think that's what people respect about him," says David Anderson, a longtime friend and member of Willie's recording studio staff.

Immediately after word spread that the IRS had seized everything, an Austin friend called to offer Willie and his family a place to stay for as long as it took to sort things out. Ultimately, Willie did not have the means to protect his extended family and his crew, many of whose members had been with him for decades.

It was going to be a long and hard struggle back. But after the initial shock of the property seizures passed, Willie decided he was going to make the fight. The first thing he did was sell his music company to a Japanese investment firm. The sale of the royalty rights to his songs earned over two million dollars, but it deprived him of the future steady income he had worked all his life to achieve. By the time he had used the proceeds of that sale to satisfy debts against the company and some portion of his tax bills, Willie had a net loss from the sale.

He soon found that he could not even continue performing on the road. It cost money to haul himself, his band, and his technicians to the shows. Each time he scheduled a performance the Feds were likely to be there to seize the entire gate—even before the bills were paid.

"During that period of time it was rough for the guys because they didn't have any money coming in," Willie recalls. "It was difficult for me, too, because I loved to play. Not knowing what was going to happen was a little bit scary."

It was damned if you work, damned if you don't. Because of this dilemma, which many delinquent taxpayers have experienced, there seemed no way to try to pay off the tax liens, or even to earn a living. As a result, Willie's music came to a halt, and for eight months he and his troupe were practically idle. He made only one album early in 1991, *Waylon and Willie—Clean Shirt.*

Just because he couldn't work did not mean that he wasn't busy. He and his attorneys were frantically trying to come up with solutions that would pay off his tax debt and let him get back to the job of making music.

They came up with a unique proposal, and to everyone's surprise, the IRS accepted it. Willie would go into a musical partnership with the Internal Revenue Service. He would try to get out of the jam the only way he knew to handle any problem—with his music. The government and Willie negotiated the $32 million tax debt down to $16.7 million: $6.7 million in taxes and $10 million in penalties.

Willie cut *Who'll Buy My Memories (The IRS Tapes)* in 1991. But before Nelson got anything from the new album, the government took the lion's share.

And the IRS would keep the books on the project.

"I don't think they trust my bookkeeping," Willie quipped. "I don't know why they should."

MUSICAL INSTRUMENTS, RECORDING EQUIPMENT, AND ALL THE TOOLS THAT WOULD HAVE ENABLED WILLIE TO CONTINUE TO WORK WERE CONFISCATED.

The recording did well, but there was no way any record album was going to pay off a debt as huge as the one filed against Willie. His lawyers also instituted lawsuits against some of his financial accountants and advisors, in an effort to recover part of the money he had lost on the tax shelters the IRS had denied.

But these efforts were not good enough and the Feds were impatient. The IRS scheduled tax auctions against his personal property and real estate. Everything was going on the block.

Just as it seemed Willie was approaching the darkest hour at the bottom of the financial pit, a strange thing began to happen.

The American farm community rallied to their beneficiary for the years of selfless benefit work he had given them through Farm Aid. *Time* magazine called the legion of farmers who came flocking to his aid "Willie's comrades-in-coveralls." The farmers knew what it was like to have their homes, tools, and livelihood seized and sold out from under them. The farmers and other fans were not going to let this happen to their old friend. Not if they could help it.

First there was an auction of all of the memorabilia, instruments, and recording

AFTER THE GOVERNMENT SWEEP, WILLIE WAS LEFT STANDING ALONE ALMOST LIKE THE YOUNG MAN WHO HAD WALKED OFF THE FARM IN ABBOTT, TEXAS, SOME FORTY YEARS EARLIER. AGAIN, IT WAS WILLIE AND A BEAT-UP OLD GUITAR AGAINST THE WORLD

equipment seized by the IRS. A group of fans mobilized a Willie Nelson and Friends Showcase and saved most of his posters, gold and platinum records, and musical instruments by purchasing everything for $7,000. The members of the Hendersonville, Tennessee, organization said they would hold these personally priceless items for Willie and his family until the tax mess was straightened out.

Then the man who had donated his time to more than one hundred benefit performances in the previous two years before his trouble began became the subject of dozens of benefit performances himself. They were small events, but nevertheless heroic. Austin declared a special Willie Nelson Appreciation Day; old friends held fund-raisers across the country. A honky-tonk owner where Willie once performed raised several thousand dollars from his customers. Willie Nelson funds were established at Waco and at tiny Abbott. Even a small-town barber set up a collection box to help out. But all these efforts could not come close to making a dent in the staggering IRS bill.

In late January 1991, the IRS held an auction on Willie's 700-acre ranch, where his home was located. The auction drew no bids. Later, a West Texas farm couple met the minimum bid for the homestead and held title until Willie was able to purchase it back from them.

That was the same month the farmers poured into Hays County to stop the auction of Willie's small farm at Dripping Springs.

Daughter Lana, who had been living on the property, was as amazed as Willie at the outpouring of generosity from fans and friends all over the United States, many of whom they had never met.

Lana recalls the dramatic turn of events:

"The farmers put together enough money to buy the house I lived in. And they bought it at one of the auctions at the courthouse . . . It was just so wonderful because people came from all over, all over America. They heard about it, and they came.

"His friends also bought back his office, everything that was in his office, his gold records, his awards, you know, personal items that meant a lot to him. Things from people that he loved.

"It was very touching. It was so moving. I mean, these people who bought these things back weren't rich people. It wasn't like a bunch of rich guys came out here and bought this stuff back. It was just normal people who got together and bought whatever they could. And then they turned around and gave it back to us."

Next, the government put up for sale the old Pedernales Country Club, which housed

Willie's studio and several of the homes of his employees, along with the nine-hole golf course. The minimum opening bid the IRS would accept for the property was $575,000. No one made an offer. A few months later, one of Willie's old friends and an ardent golfing buddy—Darrell Royal, the famous, longtime head coach of the University of Texas Longhorns football team—paid the IRS just over $100,000 for the

recording studio, golf course, and all the buildings. It was never publicly discussed how this property, a few years later, came back under Willie's control and use.

There was yet another test of Willie Nelson's mettle to come in that troubled year of 1991.

On Christmas Day, Nelson's thirty-three-year-old son, William Hugh Nelson, was found dead in his cabin home in rural Tennessee.

The first-born son everyone affectionately called Billy had apparently died from suicide by hanging. The day of his death, Billy, who had been divorced two years before, was partying until the early morning hours. A friend had dropped him off at his cabin at about 2 A.M. The medical examiner informed the family that Billy was legally intoxicated at the time of his death.

"Drinking was Billy's problem," Lana says of the tragedy that crushed her father and came closer to bringing him down than all the troubles he had experienced with ex-wives, betrayals by associates, or the IRS combined. "It might have been different if Billy had been a happy drunk. But Billy was sad and depressed."

His father and sisters Lana and Susie had struggled for years to help Billy overcome alcoholism, with Willie even attending substance-abuse counseling sessions with his son.

Billy had tried to follow in Willie's footsteps and was a part-time songwriter. But he largely depended on Willie for his income.

Friends and family knew the death of his son had hit the normally gregarious Willie harder than anything that had ever happened to him. He would not talk to anyone about the tragedy.

That terrible year of 1991 came to a heartbreaking close for the redheaded stranger. He seemed to have weathered the storm, but a close observation would reveal a lot more white hair in his long braids and beard and deeper lines etched into the familiar face. ★

WILLIE MAY HAVE BEEN SIXTY, BUT THE REDHEADED STRANGER WAS DEFINITELY BACK.

ad Willie Nelson followed the script from one of his favorite old Western movies, it would have been time for the singing cowboy to ride off into the sunset.

But Willie was an outlaw, after all, and never did follow the scripts other people handed him. In 1992, with little left but his battered guitar, he still faced a crushing tax debt and the personal devastation of his son's death.

He was starting all over with a weekly appearance on a satellite television show and some minor engagements on the road. He released only four albums in 1992, as he struggled to once again find his footing and begin the long climb back up. There was another big difference this time—Willie would soon turn sixty. Gamblers would not have given very favorable odds for a successful comeback in a fickle entertainment business, where youth and good looks were the first qualifications. But then, few people reckoned on Willie's tenacity.

Willie celebrated his sixtieth birthday on April 29, 1993, with a new project underway that many music critics came to describe as "his best work ever." It was his 110th career album and featured an eclectic selection of country and pop solos and duets with singers from across the musical spectrum. The album was *Across the Borderline*, and it featured voice and musical contributions from Paul Simon, Bonnie Raitt, Sinead O'Connor, and Bob Dylan.

Time magazine reviewer Jay Cocks said the new album was a "singular achievement . . . [it] will fix him for good right where he belongs, among the best of American music." Ken Tucker of *Entertainment Weekly* described it as "shockingly good."

Willie may have been sixty, but the redheaded stranger was definitely back. He made four more albums in 1993, eight in 1994, six in 1995. A half-dozen new albums were in the works at all times. After a three-year movie hiatus, producers once again sought him out for roles in feature films, made-for-TV movies, and documentaries. Willie would have roles in nine more films over the next few years.

The hallmark of his return came as an

HE MADE FOUR MORE ALBUMS IN 1993, EIGHT IN 1994, SIX IN 1995. A HALF-DOZEN NEW ALBUMS WERE IN THE WORKS AT ALL TIMES.

unexpected honor that year. He achieved the recognition of his peers that only the greatest in the business attain. In 1993, Willie Hugh Nelson was inducted into the Country Music Association Hall of Fame. The hall of fame, founded by the CMA in 1961, is located on Nashville's Music Row. Inductees are selected by an anonymous panel of two-hundred electors. The honor is especially significant because each elector is a veteran of the music industry who has made a major contribution to the music business.

Willie may have been highly regarded by his fellows and absolutely loved by his fans, but he still had the burden of paying his own mountain of debts.

His determination to pay off the Internal Revenue Service was a driving force in Willie's hectic new schedule—he was not going to let his advancing years slow him down. He showed the revenuers that he was honestly trying. By early 1993, he had paid $3.5 million toward the negotiated $16.7 million tax lien.

The previous year he had spent almost as much time on his tour bus, *Honeysuckle Rose II,* as he had at home. In addition to touring more than one hundred U.S. cities, he performed in twenty-three cities in nine foreign countries in a one-month period.

On February 2, 1993, Willie's long tax nightmare came to an end. He and his wife, Annie, along with his tax lawyer, appeared in the federal building in Austin for a meeting with the IRS. Willie wore a black baseball cap. The government agreed to take nine million dollars as final settlement and offered him a payback schedule without additional interest and penalties.

EVEN THOUGH HE WAS PRESIDENT OF THE FARM AID ORGANIZATION AND CONTINUED TO SPONSOR THE BIG ANNUAL BENEFIT, ON THIS OCCASION HE HELPED UNLOAD 200 BALES OF HAY IN THE BLAZING AUGUST SUN.

A beaming Willie walked from the federal building to face a crowd of news reporters and photographers. He told the *Austin American-Statesman*, "I have really worked. I really just tried . . . to work until it was over. And today it is over."

It would take Willie a couple more years but, incredibly, his comeback was great enough that he could realize his ambition to pay the government every dime of the huge tax debt.

He would never forget what the experience had taught him about people. While others going through a similar experience might have come out bitter, Willie came out awed by the response of his friends and fans. To show he had no hard feelings, in a typical Willie gesture, he signed autographs for IRS agents and tax-office employees before he left the courthouse that day.

But it was his legion of farm friends and fans that he holds closest in his memories about those years of struggle.

"All the farmers came . . . and wouldn't let anybody buy anything," he recalled years later, still with a look of wonder on his face. "You start realizing that a lot more people know who you are, want to be friends . . . I was surprised that there were that many."

It wasn't long before Willie had a chance to once again help his friends from the farm who had so recently returned the favor. When the droughts of the mid-1990s hit Texas, he stepped off the stage of Farm Aid to offer hands-on assistance. Willie helped rally farmers from nondrought areas who wanted to donate hay to small farms and ranches where cattle were starving. He laid down his guitar to literally meet the hay trucks to help unload the donated bales.

The farmer-to-farmer relief effort began on a South Carolina farm and ended on Central Texas farms. One was near Austin, and to draw national attention to the effort, Willie was

IT WASN'T LONG BEFORE WILLIE HAD A CHANCE TO ONCE AGAIN HELP HIS FRIENDS FROM THE FARM WHO HAD SO RECENTLY RETURNED THE FAVOR.

among the volunteers unloading the hay trucks. Even though he was president of the Farm Aid organization and continued to sponsor the big annual benefit, on this occasion he helped unload 200 bales of hay in the blazing August sun.

Another event soon came along that had to please the boy from Abbott. Back in the 1950s, as a struggling young father, Nelson had worked as a vacuum cleaner salesman in Fort Worth, just to make ends meet. In 1996, Willie was invited to perform a concert with the Fort Worth Symphony. A special pops concert featuring the country music legend performing with the philharmonic orchestra was as much to honor Willie as it was a musical event.

In a special tribute to Willie the orchestra opened the concert with music from heroic adventure movies, including *The Magnificent Seven*. After the intermission the orchestra turned the stage over to Willie and his band, the Family. The event was a sellout.

Willie also returned to his roots with an album cut with his sister, Bobbie, and the Family band members. The new album, *How Great Thou Art,* featured classic gospel songs that he and Bobbie had sung and played in their small country church as children.

The rough years, particularly the death of his son, had also made Willie more aware of the important role of family in his life. He and Anne-Marie became very guarded about their preschool sons, Lukas and Jacob. The boys were shielded from the press, and no inquiring paparazzi were allowed to photograph them. Every morning that Willie was not on tour, he personally got up early to have breakfast with his sons before taking them to school.

While Willie played golf as often as possible with his friends from Austin and visiting friends from all over the country, his work schedule slowed only slightly.

One institution he had to rebuild was his annual Fourth of July Reunion. Like his other activities, this popular event had lapsed in the early 1990s, due to his troubles with the IRS.

When Willie wasn't on tour he sometimes drove down from his hilltop home the few miles to a tiny hamlet called Luckenbach to play dominoes with the old-timers. He and Waylon had made the little town almost legendary with their 1977 number one single, "Luckenbach, Texas." There really was such a place, and Willie really did hang out there.

Luckenbach was an old German settlement, founded in 1849. Today, with a population of twenty-five or so, the town consists of one unpainted general store that also serves as a beer tavern, a traditional rural dance hall, and sometime blacksmith shop. On Sunday afternoons it is often the scene of spontaneous gatherings of banjo players, guitar pickers, and fiddlers. Beneath towering oak trees, old-timers teach newcomers who have moved into the popular resort communities

THE ONE THING THAT HAS NEVER CHANGED IN THE TWENTY-FIVE YEARS SINCE THE PICNICS WERE STARTED BY WILLIE IS THE STAR ATTRACTION: WILLIE HIMSELF.

of the Hill Country how to whittle and pitch washers.

It was Luckenbach where Willie decided to settle his traditional reunions for keeps. In 1995, this tiny, out-of-the-way town in the heart of the Hill Country he loved became the site for the Willie Nelson Fourth of July Picnic. While the crowds are not as large as for some past events, they still attract the diehard old hippies, a smattering of cyclists, redneck cowboys, and upscale university students. The affairs are more family-oriented now, but just as rollicking as in the days when pot smoking and skinny-dipping characterized the blistering hot midsummer event.

Luckenbach, which is located eighty miles west of Austin and no nearer any other major city, had to be a personal choice made by Willie himself. The location would not appear to be a good one for a commercial enterprise. But its first year there, the festival drew a paying crowd of more than 15,000.

"The consensus was . . . it really captured

the spirit of what the picnics are supposed to be," event promoter Tim O'Connor told a local news reporter.

The one thing that has never changed in the twenty-five years since the picnics were started by Willie is the star attraction: Willie himself. These events, more than any others, invigorate Nelson. Each year he is joined for the twelve-hour show by a score of top names in country, pop, and rock music. Willie really lets his hair down and stays onstage for the entire event.

Writing about the performance at the 1997 show, *Austin American-Statesman* music critic John T. Davis called the gathering "the cult of the Red Headed Stranger" and said its founder was "Saint Willie." Davis wrote:

"At an age when many artists have entombed their work in CD box sets (funny how much those things look like coffins . . .) and content themselves with collecting royalty checks, Nelson still displays an energy, an imagination, and a restless curiosity that is the envy of musicians half his age."

The writer, who has covered many of the annual events, said there could never be greater, all-time classics than Willie's "Crazy," "Night Life," "Hello Walls," "Funny How Time Slips Away," and "Angel Flying Too Close to the Ground."

As he grew older, Willie never forgot those who had been loyal to him in the past. In 1997, Willie and those first friends were featured on a "songwriters special" on *Austin City Limits*. Willie, Waylon, and Kris no longer needed the help of the nonprofit program, but they continued to support the PBS effort.

Nelson, who has no serious challengers, seems to keep trying to compete with and best himself, even after passing age sixty-five. In 1998, for the first time since he took control of his own music, he entrusted himself to another producer for an innovative new musical project. Producer Daniel Lanois asked him to make an

artistic stretch in the album *Teatro,* which featured inspirational music with an Afro-Latin flavor. Emmylou Harris joined Willie in some of the songs on that unusual musical adventure. Critics said the new album was a strong follow-up to Willie's successful *Spirit* album, released in 1996.

At the same time, Willie released two other brand-new productions. With a reincarnation of his old Offenders band, which he jokingly called "the repeat offenders," he released *Me and the Drummer.* And in a return musical appearance with Johnny Cash, he released *VH-1 Story Tellers.* He and Cash had shared a billing the previous year at the Westbury Music Fair, in which they proved that their combined seventy-five years of music-making cemented their roles as American music icons. They performed to standing ovations for more than three hours.

Then in August 1998, an announcement was made that thrilled the country music world. Willie Nelson was named as a distinguished honoree of the prestigious Kennedy Center in Washington, D.C. He and several other entertainers were to be honored for a lifetime of achievement in the performing arts.

Two days after Christmas 1998, Willie donned his version of formal attire—which included black cowboy hat and boots—for one of the very rare occasions he agreed to change out of his faded jeans and vest for a tux and cummerbund. He wore black velvet ribbons to tie his white-flecked, long red braids.

Willie was escorted into the nation's most magnificent arts center, past applauding fans that included Senate Majority Leader Trent Lott, Dennis Hopper, Senator Edward Kennedy, Secretary of State Madeleine Albright, Alan Greenspan, former U.S. Senators Howard Baker and Nancy Kassebaum-Baker, Jack Lemmon, Michelle Lee, and other celebrities of international stature. Seated in the audience

was another couple that had long been fans of the Texas singer—President William Jefferson Clinton and First Lady Hillary.

That night, Willie was in the unfamiliar position of being entertained by others, but many of the songs were his and were performed by friends. Kris Kristofferson belted "On the Road Again" to a stomping, clapping crowd of formally dressed dignitaries. Dwight Yoakam offered "Hello Walls." Lyle Lovett sang "Night Life" and Shelby Lynne took the audience back to Willie's earliest success with "Crazy."

Walter Cronkite anchored the extravaganza and narrated a video of Willie's career.

"Willie is a Texan whose dust-bowl voice and songs in the neon night made him a Walt Whitman of our time," the former CBS anchorman said.

Willie was presented the distinguished seven-ribbon Kennedy Center Honors medal. It was draped around his neck where the trademark red bandanna would normally be worn.

Along with Willie, other entertainers were similarly honored that evening: Shirley Temple Black, Bill Cosby, Andre Previn, Broadway composer John Kander, and lyricist Fred Ebb.

But in Texas, all eyes were on the country boy who had "done so well" in the big city. As an added attraction to the gala, Willie's tour bus, *Honeysuckle Rose II,* had been driven onto the huge, reinforced stage as a prop for the nationally televised event.

In concluding the presentation to Willie, fellow Texan and screen star Tommy Lee Jones commented that the redheaded stranger "knows who he is" and "knows where he's from, and that big bus is always going back to the Hill Country."

After being awarded the most distinguished honor a grateful nation had to give a performing artist, Willie did board that bus and was on the road again, headed back to Texas. ★

AT THE DAWN OF A NEW MILLENNIUM, WILLIE IS STILL ON THE MOVE.

Life has been a roller-coaster ride for Willie Nelson, but he has been too busy writing songs and singing about it to complain.

"I really learned that everything seems to happen for the best," he observes. "Things work out usually the way they're supposed to."

Willie Nelson has lived a life, and devoted his career, to one principle—being true to himself and what he believes to be right. In his sometimes controversial life, others may not have always agreed that his truth was the right way. But no one questions that he has stuck to his guns.

"I value the truth," Willie maintains. "I think the truth is probably the most important value that you can have."

His closest friends attest to Willie's lifetime adherence to his values, both in his dealings with others and in his career.

"Willie is probably the most centered artist I know," says lifelong friend Kris Kristofferson. "He's changed the least in the time that I've known him."

Willie counts even the turbulence in his early marriages as a plus. "There's no such thing as an ex-wife, there's only additional wives," he says. "I've learned that. And that's not necessarily a negative, either, because I'd rather have an ex-wife who's a friend than an ex-wife who's not a friend."

But one thing about his relationships is certain—the love affair with his army of fans has never wavered. He is adored by fans as much for his careful nurturing of their loyalty as for his music, as evidenced by the hours he spends after every performance signing autographs and mixing with the audience.

He has become an innovator on the Internet, reaching out to his fans through on-line chats, as well as introducing new songs to a still-emerging, worldwide audience. While Willie is a child of the Depression Era, and of the pre–baby boom generation, he is forging ahead into the new century and millennium as one of the visionaries of the industry.

Willie Nelson started the year 2000 with approximately two hundred albums to his credit, recorded over the almost half-century since he pressed the "No Place for Me" single in 1956. He has been in the forefront of the changing music scene in America, actually leading the way for many of the innovations.

An award presented to Willie a decade ago, which might not count among the grandest he has received, may be the most appropriate. In 1991, the Academy of Country Music honored him with the Pioneer Award.

He has been a pioneer, blazing trails for new generations of singers who have become country music superstars. They could never have reached the extraordinary heights in American music they achieve today if Willie and a few of the "outlaws" had not ventured to break down the old barriers between country and mainstream music years ago.

Today, country music is as mainstream as pop, jazz, rock, or blues. A major reason for this broad acceptance was Willie's early innovations in mixing rock and country to help create the progressive country sounds that have won millions of new fans.

Willie has always believed that America really is a mixing pot of races, cultures, creeds, and ethnic groups, and that the nation is stronger for it. For nearly sixty years he has used music to speak for him and has dared to venture into the unexplored to prove his point.

He has proven in his music and his life that he can constantly change, but remain the same. In the process, he has kept alive the best traditions of the past, preserving the folk culture of country music in formats that are forever young. In the closing years of the twentieth century, Willie was still experimenting with his music and pioneering trails to reach the coming generations in the information age.

He was one of the first musicians to recognize the potential of cable television as a tool for reaching new audiences, and its value as a marketing vehicle. The country music icon was the first major entertainer to sign up with the QVC shopping network—a round-the-clock program shown on more than 4,000 cable systems nationwide—to play his songs and sell his albums live to the viewing audience.

Minutes after he went on the air, the phones were ringing off the walls, and operators were taking orders for his CDs and cassettes, souvenir vests and Western shirts, and biographical video. When everything had sold

WILLIE HAS ALWAYS BELIEVED THAT AMERICA REALLY IS A MIXING POT OF RACES, CULTURES, CREEDS, AND ETHNIC GROUPS, AND THAT THE NATION IS STRONGER FOR IT.

out in about forty minutes, Willie winked at the audience and said, "I really look at myself as a salesman of music." Even after most of the items were gone, the buyers were calling in asking for Willie to sing more songs, which he did.

Another use of new technology that has expanded Nelson's reach in the information age was the recent founding of his own cable network. The Outlaw Music Channel, launched in 1998, is a showcase of vintage country and Western music shows drawing on his own huge collection of old classics. The twenty-four-hour satellite television broadcast also features Native American–themed programming, in cooperation with the Kickapoo Indian tribe of Kansas.

Willie says the channel could run for months and never repeat the same material twice. He has acquired a huge collection of

TODAY, COUNTRY MUSIC IS AS MAINSTREAM AS POP, JAZZ, ROCK, OR BLUES A MAJOR REASON FOR THIS BROAD ACCEPTANCE WAS WILLIE'S EARL INNOVATIONS IN MIXING ROCK AND COUNTRY TO HELP CREATE THE PROGRESSIVE COUNTRY SOUNDS THAT HAVE WON MILLIONS OF NEW FANS

shows from the 1960s and 1970s, which have become a part of country and Western history. His collection includes 700 episodes of *The Porter Wagoner Show* and 350 segments of *The Wilburn Brothers Show*. He also plans to air segments from many of his own early appearances and performances of his old Outlaw and Highwaymen sidekicks.

As 1999 drew to a close, Willie was booked solid. He had nearly a hundred live performances scheduled, from the Gulf Coast in Louisiana to Wisconsin on the Canadian border; from Las Vegas in the West to New York City on the East Coast.

And he was still experimenting with his recording sound, too. A 1999 album entitled *Willie Nelson Night and Day* was considered another daring risk for Willie—it was his first offering of an all-instrumental set of songs featuring his guitar-playing in duets with fiddler Johnny Gimble.

In this busy schedule in the last year of the nineties, Willie stopped long enough to help the old-timers at Luckenbach celebrate that hamlet's sesquicentennial. That 150th anniversary celebration was highlighted on the occasion of Willie's Annual Fourth of July Picnic—the fifth to be held in that tiny town. It was a show billed as "the most eclectic" gathering of performers in the two decades Willie has held his Reunion, with forty performers scheduled for another twelve-hour gala, before an estimated crowd of 15,000.

While this outdoor concert venue is one of Willie's pioneering efforts, he was also recently among the leaders in another innovative music-marketing venue—music via the Internet.

Nelson was among the first, if not the first superstar, to release a new CD exclusively on the Internet—*Tales Out of Luck*. Since Willie tried out the new marketing approach, dozens of other singing stars have begun to explore this important new medium as a profitable way to maintain more control over their artistic work and realize a larger share of the proceeds.

Willie had already been one of the first country entertainers to venture into the high-tech area of interactive CD-ROM when he released *The Life and Music of Willie Nelson* in 1996. With video and audio snippets from his life, and interviews with a number of his close associates, the interactive CD covered much of his musical life, with a dozen full songs and lyrics to thirty-two others in the ten hours of material.

For Willie there seems to be no barriers he has not already broken or walls left for him to scale on the road he travels. If something new pops up in the coming millennium, more than likely he'll be game to try kicking it down, too.

Reflecting on his journey on the road so far, Willie believes he has always been simply a songwriter and singer.

"I write a lot of sad songs. I write a lot of happy songs. I'm just a writer, and that's what I do."

And Willie says he has no plans to stop. Singing and songwriting are a way of life, not a job to him, so there's no reason for him to think about retiring.

The lines from another of his songs, "I'm Waiting Forever, for You," tells it like it is with Willie:

You are the road. You are the only way.
I'll follow you for ever more. We don't run,
and we don't compromise. We don't quit.

At the dawn of a new millennium, Willie is still on the move. Fellow travelers should not be surprised to run across a redheaded stranger carrying a beat-up old guitar slung over his shoulder, hitching down the Internet superhighway to some new horizon.

It will be Willie Hugh Nelson, slightly more weathered and gray, but simply "On the Road Again." ★